Helen McCabe is founder and managing director of Future Women. She began working in radio and television in Adelaide before moving to the Canberra Press Gallery with the Seven Network. In 2004 Helen was appointed night editor of *The Australian* newspaper, and later deputy editor of *The Sunday Telegraph*, and also spent six years as editor-in-chief of *The Australian Women's Weekly*, winning a number of industry awards including editor of the year. She is one of the few women to deliver the Andrew Olle Media Lecture. Helen is active in the not-for-profit sector, holding a series of board roles, and also held senior executive roles at Nine before launching Future Women in 2018.

Jamila Rizvi is chief creative officer for Nine's Future Women and a bestselling author for adults and children. She is an opinion columnist for the Nine newspapers and hosts two podcasts, *The Weekend Briefing* and *Anonymous Was a Woman*. Jamila has advised governments at the highest levels on gender equality, childcare, media and employment. She was named in the *Australian Financial Review*'s 100 Women of Influence and is a 2020 Women and Leadership Australia award winner.

Work.
Love.
Body.

FutureWomen

Edited by Helen McCabe and Jamila Rizvi

Work.

by Jane Gilmore

Love.

by Santilla Chingaipe

Body.

by Emily J. Brooks

hachette AUSTRALIA

Work. Love. Body. was conceived of, written, and edited on Aboriginal land. We acknowledge and pay our respects to elders of the Wathawarung, Dja Dja Warrung, Boonwurung and Wurundjeri people of the Kulin Nation, to the Gadigal people of the Eora Nation and the Kaurna people of the Adelaide Plains.

Some of the names of people in this book have been changed to protect their privacy.

Work. Love. Body. is supported by the Judith Neilson Institute for Journalism and Ideas.

Published in Australia and New Zealand in 2021
by Hachette Australia
(an imprint of Hachette Australia Pty Limited)
Level 17, 207 Kent Street, Sydney NSW 2000
www.hachette.com.au

A catalogue record for this book is available from the National Library of Australia

ISBN: 978 0 7336 4730 7 (paperback)

Cover design by Christabella Designs
Cover illustrations courtesy of Getty Images
Typeset in Adobe Garamond Pro by Kirby Jones
Printed and bound in Great Britain by Clays Ltd, Elcograf S.p.A.

The paper this book is printed on is certified against the Forest Stewardship Council® Standards. McPherson's Printing Group holds FSC® chain of custody certification SA-COC-005379. FSC® promotes environmentally responsible, socially beneficial and economically viable management of the world's forests.

To the Future Women team, who stepped up and got the job done, during a year like no other.

With thanks to the Judith Neilson Institute for their generous support of this work.

Contents

Introduction by Jamila Rizvi • 1

Work. by Jane Gilmore • 21

Love. by Santilla Chingaipe • 97

Body. by Emily J. Brooks • 183

Conclusion by Helen McCabe • 253

Appendix: The Gender Pay Gap • 271

Endnotes • 277

Acknowledgements • 291

Introduction

Jamila Rizvi

At the end of 2020, just before Christmas, my family took a long car trip. We drove for seven hours from Melbourne to Canberra to celebrate the end of an atrocious year with the people we'd barely seen throughout it. Christmas itself was a muted affair. We so urgently wanted the celebration to be special, to mark the time we'd lived through and survived. But how do you mark the end of something before it's 'over' and before you even know what 'over' looks like. And how do you reconcile the hugely different experiences of the individuals who are present? There were those who had lived in the so-called Covid Capital of our country and endured one of the world's longest and harshest lockdowns. And there were also those for whom daily existence barely changed. *Pass the prawns please. Another slice of pie? Shall we do the crackers now? Don't eat Santa's leftover milk and cookies, it's not Covid-safe.*

For me, 2020 was not unlike one long, awful car trip. We didn't do anything much except try to pass the time. We barely moved our bodies, yet we were constantly exhausted. It was as if real life had been put on pause. But unlike the entire Netflix catalogue, which we watched in lockdown, there was no option to rewind and relive the delights of what had come before. No option to fast-forward to a more comfortable place. No time stamp to tell us how long this movie might last. We stayed awake at night, wracked with insomnia, captivated by the repetitive, monotonous, terrifying uncertainty. And I know that this life pause existed not only for those living in Melbourne, for whom the world became so small when it was made to fit inside the desk drawer of a cramped makeshift home office. Rules and regulations kept us enclosed in that tiny space. We had no choice. We were wedged. While restrictions and the severity of government intervention in our lives did differ, a pause was the lived experience of all Australians.

International borders were closed. Planes grounded. Holidays cancelled. A once globalised world was declared off limits until further notice. The precious safety of our island home was guarded with unflinching enforcement. One case. Four close contacts. And state borders slammed shut. While cities went quiet and highways emptied, our homes grew louder, and louder still. Filled with toddlers shouting, sobbing older siblings, exasperated aunties, frustrated dads, and mums just trying to block it all out while trying to multitask homeschool and a Zoom presentation for work. Even the most expansive of living rooms became overcrowded with unfinished craft projects, exercise equipment and discarded paper bags of Uber Eats. Days of the week blurred together, like that period between Christmas and New Year, but without the joy. We ate and ate and ate and ate because it was the only effective method of blocking out the news.

No matter how 'normal' life might have seemed in some places, our freedom to travel, gather and be entertained as we once did was curtailed. The simplicity of meeting a friend for coffee, hugging them on arrival and smiling at the barista as you paid your bill disappeared. For a time there, cafés ceased to be places where we might congregate and instead became transactional, muted and masked. We visited the same local places most days during lockdown, trying to share our custom equally and keep every business afloat. On one occasion, my husband and I had an almost-argument over who would make the daily pilgrimage for coffee, and thus have the privilege of conversing with another adult. The warm embrace of someone we cared about was truncated to only those we lived with. (And most of us were downright sick of them.) We got lonely. Especially when it came to our thoughts of the future, no longer bright and shiny but muted and unclear.

Smiling at someone who served or helped you, the simplest of friendly courtesies, was rendered impossible. Tyra Banks, the supermodel who once hosted series upon series of a television show teaching doe-eyed, impossibly beautiful girls to pose for the camera, used to tell them to smile with their eyes. To 'smize'. I remember practising the smize in front of the mirror in my parents' bathroom because it had the best lighting. It's harder than you think. My intensity looked angrier and more manic than friendly or sexy. The smize was an act that took on a new everyday meaning for communities whose every public interaction was now masked. Something once worn only by doctors and people working with dangerous chemicals became mandatory for the rest of us, rapidly morphing into another fashion item to be personalised and bedazzled. I still want a sequined mask and I make no apology for that.

With suburbs and towns, cities and states all locked down, there were days when it seemed our economy was in freefall. Economic warnings for the future ranged from dire to total devastation. There was one night I barely resisted throwing the remote control across the room when a financial forecaster on the news used the term 'unprecedented' three times in his two-minute bulletin. Those who still left the house to work walked through empty streets to catch empty trains home to empty neighbourhoods at the end of a lonely day's labour. Deemed 'essential workers', these individuals were spared the monotony of home but at the cost of exposure to an invisible virus. It was more than enough to unsettle the mind and suffocate the soul. Everything and everyone felt dangerous.

My husband and I were some of the lucky ones who could remain employed at home. But even we found new challenges; fighting for desk space to work, mental space to homeschool, and emotional space to be alone with our worrisome thoughts. Our perfectly good-sized home felt smaller, like the walls were closing in. I missed coming home at the end of my day and telling my husband what had happened over dinner or a glass of red wine. Now he already knew about my day. It was entirely the same as his.

And then there were the citizens who lost their jobs without any real prospect of finding new ones. For some, there was JobKeeper, a fair payment to keep you going but with no promise of how long it might last. For others, there was nothing. Public universities buckled under the pressure and performers threw their hands up in despair. No help and no hope. A generation of thinkers and artists left behind.

The Covid-19 experience was not one of physical ill-health for most Australians. A little over 0.002 of us[1] actually contracted the disease. At the time of writing, only twenty-nine in every one million Australians had died from Covid. Compared to most of the world, we have fared extraordinarily well. We are the fortunate few. We are safe. Those Australians who will suffer the long-term physical effects of this virus are few and a world-class medical system will be there to support them when they need it. While the vaccine rollout bungles prompt eye rolls and shudders, there is a quiet community confidence that we'll be okay in the end. That the lucky country will remain so. That when faced with enormous global upheaval and a threat that could have killed hundreds of thousands, we have found our way through. Surely, our cleverness will not run out. Will it?

The mental health of the Australian community is another question entirely. The functionality, availability and cost of mental health care stands in stark contrast to our physical health supports. Calls to crisis lines grew[2] as Australians fought the loneliness of lockdown and sought consolation for their bubbling fears. Among the worst affected were those who had lost jobs, younger people and healthcare workers. Those without work asked where more was going to come from in an economy that was morphing into a new shape before our very eyes. Young people repeated clichés about the best years of their lives over and over in their heads as they poured their love and troubles into a device. Frontline workers compartmentalised the horror they'd witnessed and tried to save their internal agony for another day. Subsidised psychology appointments were made more plentiful by governments, but this generosity didn't last. As Australians grapple with what is hopefully the aftermath of their acute experiences of the pandemic, many will be unable to access the health care they need.

Being at home proved harder than expected. With work and kids and pets and parents and plants and homeschool and online Pilates and streaming and sourdough, there was so little time to just be. While some were ambitious, others planned to relax and rest. Everyone was disappointed. I went through a short but intense sourdough phase before my starter, Carol Breadkin, ended up in the bin where she belonged. I crafted in the best way I could, throwing intense energy at entertaining my kid who would have preferred cartoons. I scowled at my husband when he walked in front of my online HIIT class while privately thankful for an excuse to stop lunging for just a few moments. Yes, our relationships were tested. Nearly to breaking point. Others, already broken, meant there were women trapped alone at home with a person who hurt them. Stay home. Stay safe. No advice is a catch-all.

Living alone could be empty and cruel. Imagine day upon day, month on month, trapped in an apartment. Pacing the same stretch of carpet and yearning for human company. Those of us with little ones gathered them up in our arms and held them close. We wondered how this would be for them, how long it would last, how long the after-effects would shape their world and their very beings. I watched my son rocket skywards during lockdown. One night, as I lay in his bed, stroking his back and listening to his complaints of growing pains, I cried a bit. I wondered if I was growing too. If my husband and friends were growing from this experience. Or if we were just hardening to a new, bleak reality.

Those with older loved ones lived with the unease of what fate might serve to those whose frailty was clear. With visitors banned from nursing homes and restricted from being in hospitals, expressing love became more complicated. We messaged. We called. We wrote letters and baked muffins. Substitutes for the hugs and kisses we reserved for safety's sake.

Together we waited – apart but not alone – for it to be over.

Without an end date, the expanse of time between the way things were and the way things might become loomed large on a painfully distant horizon. In the midst of lockdowns, questions of mask varieties, vaccine production, and 'will we ever … again?' dominated community consciousness. Australians soon reached a common understanding. We knew we weren't going back to the old way of doing things – too much of it was no longer fit for purpose. We had learned new ways. Some of them, we even liked better. Nonetheless, we were yet to transition to a new place. We received ever-changing signals about timelines from leaders and health authorities. There were so many false starts on what turned out to be false ends. The dawning of a new year, we thought, would bring about that change. Despite the best efforts of our logical brains, we had somehow convinced ourselves that 2020 would be the end of it. Or at least the beginning of the end. Surely a time would come eventually at which we could declare 'this bit' over and move on to the next challenge. To rebuild, remake and renew. We believed deep down that a change of the Julian calendar would be it. We'd press play again and leave our world of pause behind. So when the clock struck midnight on 31 December 2020, there was a mass of dashed expectations.

Viruses, of course, do not respect clocks and calendars. Just as they do not respect state borders, periods of mourning, or the birthday party of a child who has been religiously counting down. To find an equilibrium once more. Painfully, Covid-19 gave us no such certainty. Even with multiple vaccines in production worldwide, all being rolled out with incredible speed, there was no assurance of what tomorrow would bring.

This sense we all experienced in the awfulness of 2020 and beyond, of having left something behind but not yet arrived at the new place, is called 'liminal time';[3] the in-between. Liminal time is a period of transition. Of course, the coronavirus pandemic was not the first occasion that many Australian women have been in a place of liminality. What could better characterise a phase of enforced waiting to move from one way of being to the next than pregnancy? For women who have borne children, those long 40 weeks or so of wandering, dreaming, heaving and short breathing are the very definition of liminality. Once past a certain point, there is no going back, but at the same time, one cannot speed up in the pursuit of the destination. While we like to think it's possible to plan and prepare for what's next, we must also simply exist. We must occupy the place, the body, we are in. Trapped in liminality, a state of unrest between one way of being and the next.

For more than eighteen months, the world has been in flux, with each of us experiencing a kind of functional disorientation. But while we wait for the pandemic to be over – whatever 'over' means – our world beyond it is already being fashioned. What final shape it will take remains up for discussion and debate. One thing we know for certain is that here in Australia, we have a head start. There is no question that having come through the pandemic comparatively untarnished, we have an incredible opportunity. An opportunity to 'build back better', as the politicians tell us. Looking backwards should be for the purpose of imagining better, not reminiscing about a past through rose-coloured glasses. Our lens should be squarely on the economic policy and social settings that enable a future worth inhabiting. To build an Australia that is ready for the multitude of challenges that lie ahead. An inclusive Australia that provides opportunities for every citizen, not just the privileged few. It is time for our period of liminality to come to an end. It is time to rebuild.

At the forefront of that process must be the equality of women. Women went into the pandemic already faced with a hugely unequal set of circumstances, and the pandemic has made those circumstances even more acute. Globally, women's jobs were 1.8 times more vulnerable in the pandemic than men's jobs. Women make up just under 40 per cent of the world's paid workforce but suffered 59 per cent of the job losses.[4] In Australia, women were the first workers to be laid off and the first to be rehired, often at a lower pay rate than before. Recruiters reported a change in priorities among women who returned to the labour market after lockdowns. Instead of picking up where they left off, both position and pay-wise, more women took lower-paid roles[5] for the sake of security and flexibility.

According to the Australian Institute of Criminology, almost one in ten women experienced violence from their intimate partner between March and May 2020. For a third of those women, it was the first time this had happened.

Women continued to shoulder the overwhelming burden of unpaid care work despite men being at home in greater numbers than ever before in the nation's history. Provisional results of a survey by the University of Melbourne[6] suggest that in households with children, parents are putting in an extra six hours a day of care and supervision, with women taking on more than two-thirds of the extra time. Australian Bureau of Statistics survey data[7] reveals that women were more likely than men to feel restless, nervous, lonely and like nothing could cheer them up during the lockdowns.

A whopping 37 per cent of young women aged 18–24 reported experiencing suicidal thoughts. 2020 has exposed and deepened existing inequalities, revealing the frightening precariousness of Australian women's security and happiness. Women are more likely to be socio-economically disadvantaged and live in poor housing conditions with decreased sanitation or overcrowding, which increased the likelihood they would contract and spread Covid-19. Women also make up 75 per cent of the health workforce[8] – and are more likely to work in roles that require direct physical contact with patients – placing them at greater risk of contracting the virus. In short? If the day-to-day impacts of gender inequality weren't already apparent to an individual woman, they certainly made themselves known throughout 2020.

Perhaps that's why in March 2021, nearly 100 000 people marched on the streets of Australia's cities and towns, demanding justice for women. These rallies followed extraordinary allegations of sexual misconduct and assault in the nation's parliament. They proceeded further with revelations of harassment, sexism, and abuses of power, revealing a culture of patriarchy, sleaze and recklessness in the corridors of power. That such events had allegedly taken place in Parliament House and been covered up sparked fury in the minds of women who had never set foot inside that building. The rolling allegations of February and March 2021 and the prime minister's lack of adequate response became a lightning rod for action. Women of all ages and from all walks of life – lawyers, nurses, hairdressers, university students, bloggers, athletes, schoolgirls, public servants, accountants, stay-at-home mums, hospitality workers – took it personally, for every woman alive has been harassed on the job or knows someone who has suffered harassment or worse.

I attended the Melbourne march. On a makeshift stage clumsily constructed on the back of a ute, I shouted into a dodgy microphone at thousands and thousands of my sisters and allies. I told them that I was just twenty-two years old when I started working as a government staffer at Parliament House, Canberra. That I was employed there for four years. That I grew up in a building where everyone else seemed very grown up and it wasn't until years later that I realised just how unusual the experience was. I took them back to a night when I was at a hotel bar with a dozen or so colleagues. Most of them are men. Everyone is drunk. There are two women, neither of whom I know very well, and me. We're seated together on a long couch, sitting primly with our knees together – not that there is any real alternative when wearing a skirt suit. The man, a married father, sitting on my left stands to make his goodbyes. We've been chatting for much of the night. The way he talks reminds me of my dad holding court at the breakfast table back when I was at high school, arguing as a method of preparing me for an exam.

Oozing charm, my new friend makes a point of singling out everyone in the group for individual mention as he departs.

What you have to understand is how special everyone feels. This is an important guy. Being recognised by him makes us feel important too. As he walks off, I realise he's left his hotel room key on the table in front of me. Innocently, I jump up and call out his name, waving the plastic card in the air. 'I think you forgot something?' He walks slowly and deliberately back to us, coming right up close beside me to collect the card. His fingers clasp unnecessarily around mine as he leans in, face inches from my own. 'You're so naive, it's delicious,' he says. 'That was *meant* for you.' He speaks in an exaggerated faux whisper so the whole group can hear him. Everyone is looking at us. Everyone laughs. I am mortified.

I told the crowd, whose faces were full of concern and whose placards shouted for better, for more, that this was but one occasion that stands out in my memory. There were many. As a staffer, I was a young woman in a world of older men, and for many of those men, parliament was their playground. Away from their family and friends for twenty-two weeks of every year, Canberra was a place where they worked hard and played harder. I know now that I was one of the lucky ones. While I certainly experienced sexual harassment, I was not sexually assaulted. I was not raped. I was spared that indignity, that distress, that trauma and brutality and the memories that go along with it. I was spared the experience alleged by Brittany Higgins, the brave former Liberal staffer who says she was raped on the couch of Australia's then Defence Industry Minister, Linda Reynolds.

Brittany Higgins' experience and mine were not singular. Nor were they experiences confined to the walls of Parliament House. Women from all backgrounds, professions and industries have had similar experiences. Whether at home, at work or in the community, women regularly report not feeling safe. There is behaviour which comes as second nature to us that makes men scratch their heads in confusion. Behaviour, when pointed out to them, prompts anger, defensiveness, and cries of 'not all men'. We carry our keys between our fingers while walking back to the car at night. We move train carriages because a guy is looking at us in a way that feels threatening. We smile politely and decline the advances of a colleague because it will be awkward to say what we're really thinking. We shrug off the comments of a great-uncle who is excused from the consequences of his blatantly sexist remarks because of his age. We grit our teeth when the boss calls us 'sweetie' or 'darling' or 'babe', or when a colleague describes us as *ambitious* in such a way that makes clear it isn't a compliment.

Across the country, we gathered together in force to say that it happened to us. Our presence stole nightly news bulletins, dinner party conversations and Newspoll results for weeks at a time, but was there something else going on too?

I think so. Australian women loudly and proudly demanded change after a year of being taken advantage of by employers and family members and let down by governments more than ever before. Having spent close to twelve months at home teaching children, minding pets, cleaning houses and caring for elderly relatives as well as doing their paid jobs, women were fed up. Fed up with the sexism, discrimination and violence. Fed up with the deepening and darkening of inequality caused by a pandemic that pushed them to breaking point. Fed up with being treated like second-class citizens at home, at work and in the healthcare system. Fed up with being told to wait their turn or to make way for others, being taken for granted and working without adequate thanks, let alone adequate pay. Women want misogyny, and the violence and inequalities that are borne from it, to end.

It is a rare moment in modern history that would galvanise women in such numbers, and it deserves closer inspection. It is worth noting that it took a collective experience to spur women on. No longer content with dreaming alone, women are daring to want – and to demand – aloud. That work is valued according to its worth and not which gender dominates the ranks of its employees. That work is secure, safe and flexible. For those for whom work can be difficult at times, or even impossible, a basic, livable income whose cost is borne by all of us. A balance between paid and unpaid work made possible by employers with reasonable expectations. A balance facilitated by husbands and brothers, fathers and sons. A chance to be with and care for our parents as they age and require more help than before. An opportunity to spend time with friends free of pressure, guilt and competitive one-up-man-ship. The freedom to live a full life knowing that our nation's health system will catch us when we fall, whether that fall is caused by a stone in the road or a lump in our heads. A celebration of the women whose work it is to care as early childhood educators, carers for the elderly, cleaners of hospitals and nurses of the sick. Freedom from violence at work, at home and on the soon-to-be vibrant streets of our cities.

It may well be too early to use words like 'movement' or 'reckoning'. Terms as considerable as these can perhaps only be justly applied in retrospect. But there is something in the air, and as you're about to learn we stand on the precipice of genuine reform that could benefit women for generations to come. There is a decades-long whisper among the women I speak with that the work of feminism is not done yet. That while things seem fair on the surface, evil lurks beneath the waters. Women's lives remain the subject of stereotype and expectation, judgement and lack of opportunity. The pandemic has laid these realities bare in a way that is hard to ignore. The world is hurting as a whole, but women's wounds cut deep, and the blood runs thick. There is pain steeped in politics, a lack of empathy and acknowledgement, a frustration that is giving way to fury that must be channelled calmly, seriously and judiciously towards a better deal for all women. Not just for the privileged – the wealthy, the white, the abled, the straight, the cis-gendered – but for women whose stories have too long been forgotten.

Coronavirus may have brought the world to its knees. But it is women who will stand strong in its wake.

Work.

Jane Gilmore

Jane Gilmore was the founding editor of *The King's Tribune*. She is now a freelance journalist and a regular columnist for *The Age* and *Sydney Morning Herald*. Jane is currently completing a Master of Journalism at the University of Melbourne and has a particular interest in feminism, media and data journalism.

For the first time in almost a year, I can walk into a Melbourne supermarket without wearing a face mask. After so long, I feel weirdly vulnerable, almost naked, without one. It is, however, much easier to have casual conversations with strangers now we can see each other's faces again, which is exactly how I struck up a conversation with Alice* just a few weeks ago. Alice works in a suburban supermarket. When we started talking, she was laughing about the technology changes she's seen during her almost twenty years behind the cash register. 'One of the reasons I got the job is because I'm really good at arithmetic. Remember the days when we had to calculate in our heads how much change to give?' Alice was born in Australia to Asian parents, and she told me racism has always been a problem for her at work. 'I was called a "fucking boatie" on my first day and it's never really gone away. In the lockdown, one man called me a "diseased slant-eyed cunt" because I couldn't get him any toilet paper. There were days when I was scared to go to work, and I couldn't do anything about it. I didn't want to complain because I'm in my fifties now and I'm too easy to replace. I've only ever worked in retail. There's no way I'd have got another job in 2020.'

Alice's story shows how close the connection can be between racism, sexism, and poverty. The man who abused Alice went straight to racist slurs, safe in the knowledge that, as a white man, he had power that she didn't. Perhaps Alice's low-income job gave him a sense of status, that somehow his station was higher than hers and he was entitled to abuse her. It also shows how women's lives are still held hostage to the old myths about gender, race, age and sexuality that have propped up white men's power for centuries. Those myths say women are weak, emotional, best suited to subservient, nurturing roles, while men are strong, logical and best suited to leadership. They tell us women's sexuality is dangerous – we are either 'pure' or 'wicked'; either way, we are an irresistible temptation for men, who are not responsible for the lustful thoughts our bodies impose upon them, or the actions that follow. Gender myths tell us that a woman's age is an indication of her value. Sometimes I feel like we get about half an hour in our late twenties when we're actually the 'right' age. Otherwise, we're either too young to count or too old to matter.

These stereotypes are the basic foundations on which all our gendered inequalities rest. They are embedded in the political and public lives of all Australians. They are the reason women do too much unpaid and underpaid work. They are also why men don't do enough unpaid work and are paid far more than women in the job market. Women of colour, women in poverty and women with disabilities are marginalised even further. We have seen how white women are sometimes given voice and opportunity while First Nations women are ignored, or even attacked, for just trying to be part of the conversation. White male voices are still the loudest in mainstream discussion, while white women are patronised and Blak women are ignored, erased or abused.

Covid-19 didn't create these inequalities but, as always happens in a crisis, the existing fault lines were ripped wide open under the pressure of fear, loss, and the threat of a descent into poverty. Around half a million Australian women lost their jobs in 2020, the first year of the Covid-19 pandemic. While many of them did find work again in 2021, evidence suggests that they went back to work on lower incomes and were employed for fewer hours. I am writing this just after the much relied on JobKeeper payment ended. While the jobs market seems to be rebounding better than expected, wage growth is low, superannuation is unequal and women, again, are likely to be the hardest hit as those problems worsen. The once-in-a-hundred-years events are now happening every ten years, and women who were pushed further from economic security by Covid-19 will be hit again. Probably more than once. We need to clearly understand where we have come from and where we are now if we're going to ensure that Australian women don't again suffer disproportionately in the inevitable economic shocks still to come.

It happened to Alice. It happened to me. One day, it might happen to my daughter. Or to yours.

Covid-19 showed in stark detail just how essential women's work is to our collective survival and how, at the same time, it remains deeply undervalued. And yet the same old arguments that existed before Covid-19 were rolled out once again by the loudest (mostly male) voices in politics and the media after the federal budget in late 2020. The so-called Covid Budget was rightly decried for ignoring the effect of the pandemic on women. Politicians and journalists loudly proclaimed this was okay, because women and men had both been impacted by Covid-19. We were reminded that women drive on the same soon-to-be upgraded roads as men. That women also have jobs (12 per cent of them) in building and construction[9] and will benefit from the lucrative infrastructure contracts that would flow from government stimulus. We were told (again) that men have more wealth and income than women because they make different choices. Women, we were told, choose to work in low-paid industries such as childcare or aged care or nursing. That these jobs are so horrendously undervalued is not, apparently, a problem that needs to be fixed – it's just the way things are. Women also choose to have babies (and men don't?) so of course they lose income and career progression (and men don't). So why should women, who make all these poor financial choices, not bear the consequences of lower wages, stagnating careers and superannuation loss?

The World Economic Forum produces an annual measure of the global gender pay gap, comparing countries across four areas: economic participation and opportunity, educational attainment, health and survival, and political empowerment. Australia has dropped from a ranking of fifteenth in the world when this measure was first introduced in 2006, to forty-fourth in 2020. That's a drop of twenty-nine places in just fourteen years. We are falling behind comparable nations. Australian women are becoming more disadvantaged while the rest of the world is investing in improving women's lives. Economic security for Australian women must be a priority for our country as we emerge from the pandemic, or women will reap dark and dire consequences, not just now, but for many generations to come.

Thankfully, it seems like a lifetime ago that these arguments were relegated to the 'women's sections' of the news. Questions of women's safety and economic security are now mainstream, front-page news. The pandemic in 2020 and the March4Justice in 2021 changed the way Australians understand power, money and gender. Within months of being allowed to safely gather together publicly, women and non-binary people once again picked up their cudgels and started smashing away at outdated myths in ways we haven't seen since the sexual revolution of the seventies. I love the feeling of national solidarity and momentum. I hope that it can be maintained long enough to make real change, because if it doesn't, all we'll have left is despair and the status quo.

The second Covid Budget, in May 2021, was a warning sign that this possibility is all too real. While it was heavily promoted as 'the women's budget', the $3.4 billion promised on 'women's issues' remains at just over 2 per cent of the $161 billion 2020–21 deficit. Half of that spend on women ($1.7 billion) is for childcare and calling that a 'women's issue' is part of the problem. Childcare is not a women's issue. It is a parents' issue.

No one can deny the pandemic made austerity even more dangerous than usual. The government had to spend, and spend big, to keep the economy going. This was important to keep people in jobs and to keep people spending. But this budget also represented a once-in-a-lifetime chance for reform. It's high – albeit necessary – overall spending will leave Australia with over $1 trillion of debt and the government has not proposed any real plan to pay that money back. If we are going to go into intergenerational debt – that is, debt so large that future generations will be left to repay it long after we are dead – then we must spend it on intergenerational change. Papering over structural problems with superficial political cladding, hoping there's enough to cover the holes for another election cycle, is criminally wasteful.

The huge spend on childcare will be welcomed by parents and childcare centres alike. It will improve the short-term affordability of childcare for many families. This is, of course, a good thing. But it does not do anything to alter the underlying issue that early childhood education needs to be integrated into the education system as a whole rather than remain as an underfunded, glorified babysitting service. Childcare providers need to be more tightly regulated and early childhood educators need to be paid in the same way we regulate and pay any other teachers. The 2021 budget provided a needed temporary sugar hit but why didn't the government think more long term? Why not seize an opportunity to couple big spending with big reform that would reset a growing industry for the future?

The extra money for domestic and sexual violence is desperately needed, but again, is nothing more than a short-term high. It still assumes the remedy will be delivered by police and courts, even though the police can be part of the problem nearly as often as they are the solution, and the courts are issuing often-unenforced protection orders or prison sentences that focus only on punishment rather than rehabilitation.

Aged care funding was delivered on in the budget too and to an even greater dollar figure than childcare. There is no doubt that it was desperately needed. But the failures in aged care, as revealed by the Royal Commission, were as much about lack of regulation and accountability as they were about funding. Coupled with this is the absence of job security and adequate pay that would attract a committed, qualified and full-time workforce. This was yet another reminder that money without reform does not fix the problem. The spending announced in the 2021 budget was unarguably a critical first step. But the number of Australians aged over eighty-five is projected to triple in the next thirty years. Many of them will rely on residential aged care and the majority of them will be female. Billions always sounds big, but the reality is that billions will simply be wasted if there is no clear plan to fund and monitor the care older Australians will need.

It's also worth remembering that caring workforces tend to be overwhelmingly female. Aged care is no different. There was nothing in the 2021–22 budget to address the chronically low wages in female-dominated industries. Think of all the industries that tend to have a female-dominated workforce: education, professional cleaning, mental health, nursing, hairdressing. All of these industries suffer from inadequate remuneration in comparison to similar male-dominated industries.

As we come to grips with the realisation that Covid-19 was not a temporary blip but an ongoing issue the entire world will have to grapple with for years to come, we are going to have to make deep changes to our economic lives. This means we have an opportunity to dig into those structural issues and change them – permanently. The 2021 budget, while high spending, did not go far enough in this regard.

Women lost jobs, income and safety in 2020, while their unpaid labour increased considerably. The work of caring for children, homes, and vulnerable and sick family members fell mostly on women. As well as the physical and emotional toll, this burden has a significant economic effect on women – and it always gets worse in a crisis. Unpaid time spent caring and cleaning and administering households and emotionally supporting others is integral to our humanity. One of the reasons women suffer disproportionate economic insecurity is that we continue to shoulder the majority of this undervalued and unpaid work.

By contrast, Covid-19 also gave us access to flexible work in ways we never had before, and men did pick up a bit more (although still not enough) of the unpaid work every family needs to function properly. Women, who have been asking since they first walked through the doors of office buildings and factories, were suddenly able to work more flexibly. Decades of excuses and doubt about working remotely disappeared overnight and many women were finally able to access the flexibility they needed. Everything we lost and everything we gained since the beginning of 2020 tells a story.

It proves the reality of women's economic insecurity before Covid-19, and the worsening reality now. It also proves the possibility of real change – if Australians want it enough to make it happen.

For a few brief months, Australians knew what life could be like without having to pay for childcare. We lifted unemployed people and single parents out of poverty. We almost completely solved homelessness. We had a national discussion about men's violence against women and how it permeates our lives at work and at home. We saw what can happen when the entire country acts to protect our most vulnerable. It was an inspirational, if brief, glimpse of how we could be as a nation when we make safety more important than ideology. Getting back to normal life shouldn't mean forgetting the lessons we've learned about what can be possible – and better – for women.

Money is not only about buying shiny things. The old adage that money cannot buy happiness may be true, but what it *can* buy is safety, independence and choices. These things may not create happiness on their own, but it is almost impossible to be happy without them.

For nearly two hundred years, women have been fighting to be recognised as having the same political, personal and economic value as men. It doesn't always feel like it, but in the long view, we're winning that fight. Sometimes we can forget how much has changed for women, even in the last fifty years. My mother is in her seventies now. When I talk to her about what life was like when she started work as a teenager in the 1960s, I'm shocked by how different life was for me when I started work. And even more so when I compare it to what I expect for my daughter, who is about that age now.

When my mum started work, there were only two women in Federal Parliament. Australian women had not won the legal right to equal pay. Rape in marriage was not a crime, but abortion was. Australian women could not take out loans or mortgages without a man's signature. Unmarried mothers were not eligible for welfare benefits. In some states, women did not have full rights to sit on juries. No-fault divorce didn't exist. The contraceptive pill incurred a 27.5 per cent 'luxury tax' and wasn't available on the National Health Scheme. Full voting rights for Aboriginal people had only existed for five years and no First Nations people – let alone First Nations women – had ever sat in an Australian parliament. Just over fifty years later, all those things have changed significantly. But they didn't just change on their own and women weren't simply handed those changes by benevolent men. We fought – and fought hard – for them. We protested, marched, campaigned and demanded change. And it worked.

My mother has retired now, and my daughter has her first job. Covid-19 has changed their lives again. Mum is still waiting for her Covid-19 vaccine and my daughter got her job within two hours of applying because all the backpackers and international students who used to staff Melbourne's bars and cafés have vanished. My kid can make the time to do extra shifts because half of her university classes are still online. She gets the occasional leers and pick-up lines from customers, but she experiences nothing like the groping and vicious slurs I remember being standard in hospitality work when I was at university.

My mother and my daughter are very much alike. Both of them are more disciplined and organised than I will ever be. But my daughter and her mates are living very different lives to the women of my mother's generation – in part thanks to the courage the older women of today showed when they were young. Those women who fought for women's rights fifty years ago won a lot of change for us. That should give us hope for the battles to come in the post-pandemic period.

The 1970s was a time of huge social change in Australia as the women of the baby boomer generation demanded a voice and a space in public life. 'The personal is political' was a catchcry, because the difference between the public and personal prior to the seventies was so sharply gendered. Men had public lives; they were the ones with careers and professions. Men were almost exclusively in charge of governments, and they were also the ones making their mark and claiming accolades in sport and art. Women's lives were personal and private, only for themselves and each other. The Royal Commission on Human Relationships, established by Gough Whitlam, was the first time that women's personal stories were brought into the political arena in Australia. I was astonished when I read about it during lockdown, partly by how revolutionary it was for its time and partly because I had never heard about it before. Women told the Commission about their experiences of abortion, domestic abuse, poverty and family relationships. As a result, those very private, very female experiences made it to the mainstream media, which until then had been reserved primarily for men's stories. The Commission recommended, among many other things, decriminalising abortion and homosexuality. It took many years, but those things did eventually happen and, despite the doom-wailing at the time, families were not destroyed by changing our understanding of what they are or could or should be. That can happen again – and it needs to, because there is too much that remains alarmingly unchanged.

We have a new generation of young women showing up now, armed with strength and courage, ready to fight for more freedom, more safety, more change. Australian of the Year Grace Tame, who advocates so eloquently for survivors of sexual abuse. Brittany Higgins, who put a face and a story to the rampant misogyny in our Federal Parliament. Lidia

Thorpe, the first Aboriginal person elected to the Victorian parliament and now holding a seat in the Federal Senate, who fights uncompromisingly for First Nations people. These women are still making the personal political. It has been electrifying to watch their staunch refusal to accept the shame that predatory men always assume they can shift from themselves to the women they've abused. Too many of us still live with the shame that rightly belongs to the men who hurt us and far too many men in public life still don't understand that. Which is why the government failed so comprehensively to understand the power and fury of the March4Justice movement in early 2021.

Men in power will continue to misunderstand us or ignore us, sometimes wilfully and often with breathtaking animosity. We must not let them get away with it.

Women's economic lives are political as much as they are personal. It is therefore a political necessity to acknowledge that the economic horrors of this crisis haven't been doled out fairly or evenly.

My own working life has been erratic. I've had some tough times and I've also had some really good times. During one of those good times, I was working a lot of hours and had no time for housework, but I did have the money to pay for help. That's when I met Maria*, my lifesaving cleaner. Maria's family migrated to Australia from Italy when she was a teenager. Now in her fifties, Maria loves being an Australian. She describes herself as both lucky and hardworking. When Maria's father died, he left her enough money for a deposit on a small house in outer Melbourne. Still, Maria lives carefully. She has a mortgage to pay and two children living at home. For the last fifteen years, whenever Maria has a little extra cleaning work, she does a big trip to her local market and makes soups, casseroles, pies and lasagnes to fill her chest freezer. Her teenage son can get through an entire lasagne by himself, so Maria has plenty of them stacked away for him, as well as her favourite chickpea soup and the homemade cherry pies her daughter loves so much. 'That freezer was a lifesaver,' she says. 'I would make sure we always had at least two months of meals stored away so I wouldn't have to worry if I lost a couple of clients. We'd have enough food to get through until I found new ones.'

The chest freezer stopped working in the middle of 2019 and Maria couldn't afford to replace it. She kept as many lasagnes and pies as she could, but the small freezer space in her fridge filled too quickly. What she couldn't give to friends and family, she had to throw away. 'It would have been more than $500 worth of food that I lost when the freezer broke. It broke my heart.' Maria speaks to the value of the ingredients alone. But she didn't count her own labour that went into the spoiled food: her planning, shopping and thoughtful, loving cooking. This was a considerable loss, too.

When the pandemic hit, houses in Melbourne were closed to anyone but their occupants. Years of building up relationships with her clients were wiped out in a week. 'I kept a few jobs I do for people with disabilities,' Maria says, 'but most of my work disappeared. I had no savings and no food stored. I was terrified. The very first thing I did when they gave us the Coronavirus Supplement was buy a new freezer and I spent most of the lockdown filling it up. The work is coming back now, and the freezer is full, but I don't know how much longer I can keep working.'

Maria has back problems. She can't move about as smoothly or painlessly as she used to, and cleaning work requires lots of bending. This means she simply can't keep up the pace of the past and she worries it might annoy her clients. 'People don't want someone working slowly when they clean a house. They don't want me taking a break or sitting down for half an hour in their home. They want me to clean and go.' The lack of humanity in that statement is shocking but not surprising. Maria knows her work is good, but she is afraid that if she slows down, her clients will move on and find someone else. Maria has some superannuation put away, but she's fifty-five years old now, which means she can't use it for another twelve years. While she loves that new freezer, even the miraculously ingenious Maria can't fill it with enough meals for more than a decade. 'I don't know what I'm going to do if I can't keep working,' she says.

The sexist myth that domestic cleaners work for rich women who are too posh to clean a toilet is just that. And it's pretty easy to debunk if you talk to people with disabilities or any family where the adults are working full time and the kids are creating a full-time mess. According to the Australian government's Job Outlook website, around 35 000 Australians work as domestic cleaners. They're paid roughly minimum wage but rarely have employment contracts that offer the security of paid sick or annual leave. Fifty-seven per cent of the workforce, like Maria, are aged forty-five or older. Domestic cleaners are some of the lowest paid employees in the country and a whopping three-quarters of them are women.

The yawning difference between men's and women's economic security is often ascribed to the gender pay gap. While that's certainly part of it, it's not the whole story. In fact, the official gender pay gap of 13.4 per cent between the average man's full-time salary and the average woman's full-time salary isn't even the actual gender pay gap. In real terms, the gender pay gap is 45 per cent (see appendix on p. 271). This is partly due to the fact that women do too much unpaid work and men don't do enough. It's also because the richest and most powerful people in the country are men and those men tend to promote people who look, sound and act like them. Another major factor is that the jobs that pay the least are the ones done mostly by women, such as childcare, community services, administration, sales – and cleaning.

But why? Why is the work done by an early childhood educator less valuable than the work done by a carpenter? Is an electrician more important than a frontline domestic abuse worker? Does a hairdresser spend less time learning their trade than a plumber? Is a CEO really worth up to twenty times the value of an office manager? Most people's answer would be 'of course not' and yet if we go by the way these professions are paid, then the answer to each of those questions is yes. What we say means little compared with the monetary value we give to particular jobs and skills. What we pay for certain kinds of work says far more about how we think about the women who do that work than what their labour is actually worth.

When we closed down our towns, cities, societies and economies, women were still leaving the house to work. It was mostly women who sterilised and disinfected Covid-19 infection sites, who nursed patients who contracted the virus, who cared for elderly people who were most at risk and educated the children of other essential workers. Women were the workers who got Australia through the pandemic. And while we saluted them on social media with pixelated logos of helping hands, we failed to value them in the way that would have made a difference. We failed to pay them properly.

Checkout operators, who cop regular abuse from customers, are among the lowest paid workers and 75 per cent of them are women. Surgeons and anaesthetists are the highest paid people in Australia but only 18 and 33 per cent of them respectively are women. This pattern repeats itself across almost every industry and occupation. Interestingly, men who work in female-dominated industries don't always experience the same undervaluing. In fact, they tend to quickly attain seniority because it's perceived as shameful for a man to do women's work and then be told how to do it by women. The baseless perception that men manage, lead, negotiate and innovate more than women means they're often rewarded for being better and more useful, even when none of those things are true. Over 60 per cent of veterinarians are women and yet male vets, on average, earn twice as much as female vets. The nursing profession is still 87 per cent women but in 2018, male registered nurses earned, on average, almost 10 per cent more than female registered nurses. The bottom line is this: jobs that women tend to do are paid less than jobs men tend to do. And men get paid more than women for doing the same jobs. That this still happens more than fifty years after Australian women first won equal pay boggles my mind. The only reason I can find for why this fact is not leading the nightly news every day of the week is that the people in power (men) just don't think it matters.

It's deeply insulting that work fitting the traditionally female stereotype still isn't viewed as 'serious' work and is therefore not deserving of serious wages. Let's take just two examples. Hairdressing is still viewed as a vanity for women and not thought about in the same way as the so-called serious man business of pipes and sewage. After Melbourne went through one of the world's tightest lockdowns for more than 100 days in a row, the population was emotionally and mentally exhausted. And we were looking pretty shaggy. On the *7AM* podcast, journalist Rick Morton reflected on what it meant for everyone to finally leave their homes for a cut and colour. He said it was like 'a giant petri dish of a city was going to come out of itself. And one of the first lines of people who were going to mediate that kind of social response was hairdressers and barbers.' Salons were booked out for weeks within twenty-four hours of the premier's announcement that they would be allowed to re-open. The desire for a professional haircut was about more than just looking neat and tidy, it went to the core of people's identity. Morton said seeing a hairdresser 'is not just a simple transaction … They play a much bigger role in our lives. And they often act as … counsellors, trauma therapists and in some cases domestic violence or family violence referral services.' Hairdressing is about so much more than hair.

Just over 85 per cent of hairdressers are women and, on average, male hairdressers earn 10 per cent more than female hairdressers.[10]

Childcare is a routinely undervalued profession staffed almost entirely by women. It is also a service we think of as something for mothers, not fathers. Politicians talk about it as a 'women's issue', not the parents' issue it actually is. The implication being that men must go to work to support their families while women's work is just a hobby. There is an unspoken assumption that women who work in early childhood education do it because they love babies, not because they are respected professionals doing vitally important work. An occupation which, at its higher levels, requires a university degree, is regularly dismissed as 'babysitting' rather than essential early childhood education. More than 90 per cent of human brain development is thought to happen in the first five years of life and yet we assume the women who provide education services during this critical time are just playing with babies? How utterly short-sighted.

Traditionally female jobs are an extension of women's unpaid work – community service, nursing, childcare, administration, personal services, animal care, domestic work, event management, personal assistance. This not only diminishes the contribution of women and leads to lower pay, but women are also promoted less often. That is a truth I know all too well. Before I turned to journalism, I worked in the energy industry. There were very few women in the industry then, but it was still a lot of fun in many ways.

It's where I learned to work with data and spreadsheets. It's where I learned to hold my own when I was, as I almost always was, the only woman in the room. It's also where I was working the first time I was asked to train a younger, less experienced, less knowledgeable man and then watched as he was quickly promoted over me, still knowing less than I did. The second time this happened, I was old enough and confident enough to object. My boss's response was to tell me that the young man 'showed a lot of promise'. That he had a wife and children depending on him. I also had children depending on me and did not have the benefit of a wife to look after us, but that apparently was my choice, not my boss's responsibility.

For too many women, a lifetime of unpaid and underpaid work leaves them facing their later years in poverty, housing stress and loneliness. This will only be exacerbated in the years following the pandemic.

Before anyone had even heard of Covid-19, Australian women already had far less money stashed away for their retirements. Superannuation was an amazing piece of public policy when first introduced, but it was created on the assumption that women had husbands who would look after them in their twilight years. This is just not the case for many, many women. Over 20 per cent of 60-year-old women live alone and the rate of older women living alone has increased steadily since the 1940s.[11] In 2015, men in their forties had over 60 per cent higher average superannuation balances than women of the same age. Around 45 per cent of women aged fifty-five to sixty had no superannuation at all. In many cases, this will be because women have drawn down on their superannuation to pay off mortgages or other debts, but there are far too many women who could not choose a working life that built up enough superannuation to live on. Either way, most of those women will be living on the Age Pension which, at the time of writing, is just $68 per day.

I was thinking about that $68 a day when I did some grocery shopping this morning. It wasn't a big shop; just some vegetables and nuts for a stir-fry, a bag of muesli, a loaf of bread, dog food, laundry powder and a packet of Oreos for reasons I'm sure I do not need to explain. The total came to just under $45. That was before I'd paid my electricity, or phone or water bills. It didn't include the price of petrol or train tickets, nor did it allow for the cost of fixing the broken heel on my boots, new underwear, or filling a script at the chemist. It didn't include my rent. The remaining $26 a day, leftover after that basic shop, was not even going to come close to covering all those necessary items. I tried to imagine what life will be like when I am older, living alone and just trying to survive. I thought about the tiny amount of superannuation that I have, and the growing costs of health care. I have a family history of cancer and the effect of cheap running shoes on my knees means they will one day need expensive treatment. I thought about all the other women my age and older who will soon or are already facing this impossible future … and I had to go back and get another packet of Oreos.

Given that inadequate superannuation was such a problem for women before the pandemic, it was astounding that the Australian government decided to allow early release of superannuation as part of their 'assistance' package for people who lost income because of Covid-19. I'm not sure why encouraging scared people to rob themselves of a secure future was called 'assistance', but that's what they did. The consequences will be disastrous. Nearly one million people under the age of thirty-five drained their superannuation in 2020. Women in all age groups were more likely than men to withdraw their entire balance under the scheme, and women overall withdrew a greater proportion of their superannuation than men. We don't know how many of those women withdrew their superannuation at the behest of abusive partners, but we do know financial abuse is a common tactic used by violent men. If a woman has no money, now or for the future, it's much easier to control her and terrify her into staying. Forcing a woman to draw down her superannuation to zero is certainly one way to do that.

All of the women who withdrew superannuation during the pandemic will suffer for it in the long-term. A thirty-year-old woman who took $20 000 from her superannuation in 2020 could lose up to $300 000 from her balance at retirement. That's not just Oreo money. That's living costs or a fully paid mortgage or home help to stave off going into an aged care home. And what happens to a thirty-year-old woman if she took that money out because she lost her job and now can't get another one? What happens if she has children and leaves the workforce for a period and only goes back part-time, as so many women do? Suddenly she is at serious risk of poverty and homelessness. Not only now, but for the rest of her life. The options for earning money get fewer and smaller the older a woman gets. Age discrimination is a monumental barrier for women, making it much more difficult to find jobs even after they turn fifty, which is hardly old but, as Maria (lasagne maker extraordinaire) pointed out, is still seventeen years away from retirement age.

It's easy to say that people should have known better than to access their superannuation early. It's probably even true. But it's almost impossible to think sensibly about a distant future when you're in a panic about unpaid bills and the pressure of the present seems almost unbearable. I was eligible for the early superannuation access when it was first announced. I wanted to do it. My car had pretty much rusted shut. I had no paid work and no prospect of getting any in 2020.

The idea of having $20 000 to fund a slightly less rusted car and clean up my terrifyingly overdue bills seemed such an easy way out. Retirement felt like something way too far into the future to be real. It's going to happen to a different me, someone old and past it, someone I can't even imagine being. I'm so used to thinking of myself as a journalist, I can't even picture a time where I might not be able to keep writing for a living. Who will I be then, when I can't write or hustle for work or get in a car to interview someone or jump on a plane to give a speech interstate? Even worse, who will I be if I can still do those things, but everyone thinks I'm too old to do them well? The very existence of that older version of me is completely unimaginable, so I couldn't make sense of sacrificing my peace of mind for hers.

Luckily, my mother got an inkling of my intentions and firmly squashed them. Mum spent much of her working life sacrificing holidays and nights out so she could put extra money into her superannuation. The scheme was announced during Melbourne's lockdown, so I couldn't visit her to talk about it in person. We were on the phone (because Mum hates FaceTime), but I didn't need to see her face to picture her expression. I've seen it every time we've had a conversation about money. It's part horror, part bewilderment, and mostly fear. Unlike me, Mum has always been able to envision her future self. She has also learned to be patient with me and explain things slowly. On that occasion, she gently reminded me that she was not 'old' when she retired. All the work she had put into saving for retirement is the reason she has a comfortable, healthy, secure life now. It's why she can buy a good steak and a nice bottle of wine for us when I go over for dinner. It's how she affords private health insurance and good-quality orthopaedic shoes. And, as she also reminded me, time goes by so quickly. My gorgeous babies, the ones I thought would always be little, are adults now. Blink twice and they'll be coming to visit me in my retirement. I want to be able to answer the door to them in my comfortable (and attractive!) shoes. I want to be able to share a nice dinner and a glass of wine with them too. And I can't do that on $68 a day.

Many years ago, I joked to a group of mates about needing to die young because I was never going to be able to afford to retire. Thinking back on that makes me cringe. I'm not old yet, but I can see it from where I am now. There's nothing funny about dying young, and there's definitely nothing funny about being old and poor and powerless to change it.

Linh* lives in the western suburbs of Sydney and works as a children's performer. It's taken years for her to turn the thing she's most passionate about into a career. Linh admits it's not a particularly secure or well-paid job but is adamant that she wouldn't trade it for an alternative life path. This is what she loves. 'Mum and dad wanted me to be a doctor or a lawyer,' Linh told my colleague in an interview. 'It's a cliché but that's what Asian parents expect. Actress was not in any of their five-year plans for me. They gave up a lot for me and my brothers, and mum is always reminding me she didn't sacrifice so I could busk on Pitt Street with my keyboard.' When the pandemic began, Linh's show got postponed, and then postponed again, and then cancelled. The other play she'd booked later in the year was cancelled before auditions even began. 2020 began as a pretty impressive-looking calendar of work but by April, Linh had no idea what to do. 'I wasn't eligible for JobKeeper because I wasn't earning anything this time last year,' she explains. 'I tried to get a job in hospo, but all the restaurants were shut down and not hiring. When I tried to get nannying jobs, people were weird about it because they didn't want a new person in their house because of the virus. I was in a super bad spot. By May, I didn't have much choice but to move back in with Mum and Dad and suffer a 2020-long lecture about how I should have studied accounting. At least I had somewhere to go.'

During the early months of the pandemic, it was Australian women like Linh who lost more jobs, more hours and more income than their male counterparts. Research by The Australia Institute found that between March and April of 2020, the number of women employed fell 5.3 per cent compared to 3.9 per cent for men. The number of hours worked by Australian women also fell faster: women lost 11.5 per cent of their hours compared to 7.5 per cent for men. At the same time, the number of hours women spent on unpaid work increased dramatically. Women were already doing twice as much unpaid work as men before the pandemic – a fact that continually surprises men and elicits little more than tired eye rolls from women. At the height of the national lockdowns, women's unpaid work increased by about five hours a day, whereas men's increased by about half of that. There are some small variations across industries but the jobs market in Australia looks like it will return to roughly the same state it was in before the pandemic, although it may take a little longer in Melbourne. By June 2021, the unemployment rates of men and women had returned to roughly pre-pandemic levels, wages remained stagnant, and the real gender pay gap hadn't changed. Despite moments of hope and revelation during the lockdowns and periods of working at home, women continue to do most of the nation's caring work. Everything changed and yet somehow, everything stayed the same.

The Australian government's initial response to Covid-19 was uncharacteristically generous. People with young children were freed from the burden of childcare fees in a magical glimpse of what life could be like if childcare wasn't backbreakingly expensive. The introduction of the

Coronavirus Supplement swept almost everyone on Single Parent Payment, Youth Allowance and Newstart Allowance out of unsustainable poverty. All those people who had been living on the absolute margins were given time to take a breath and take stock. The ever-present threat of financial ruin and a descent into homelessness was held at bay, for at least six months, providing much-needed relief to tens of thousands of Australians who had previously been counting every twenty-cent piece. The $750 a week JobKeeper payment kept millions of Australians in jobs that they would otherwise have lost. The programs had flaws, of course, but they stopped the nation from descending into panic and prevented a far deeper recession.

I was one of the people saved by the government's initial response. I was genuinely terrified during those first few weeks of lockdown. The deluge of emails I received, cancelling speaking gigs, freelance work, contracts and workshops was fierce and fast. I lost an entire year's work in the space of two weeks. I had no idea how I was going to feed my family. The fear was eviscerating, but even more than that was grief. I had such big, ambitious plans for 2020. I had a new book proposal ready to pitch and I was going to start teaching at university. I had a calendar full of interstate trips for writers' festivals and author talks booked in country town libraries – always fun and exciting gigs. In February, I told my mother 2020 was going to be my best year yet. One month later, it had all come crashing down and suddenly I couldn't afford to pay my electricity bill. It was another reminder of how precariously even reasonably well-off people walk the line between fine and financial panic. I cried the day I found out that I qualified for JobKeeper. Not just a few delicate little tears; it was big, snotty, sheep-noise crying. The relief was indescribable. Like everyone (other than some large multinational companies), I used JobKeeper for exactly its stated purpose. It kept my business – and my family – alive until the effects of the pandemic diminished and I could get back to work.

I was certainly not alone; 3.6 million other people joined me on the JobKeeper payment, and I imagine that, like me, they were deeply grateful for it. It was an economic safety net unlike anything Australia had ever seen. There was, however, a caveat: JobKeeper was temporary. The economy, according to Prime Minister Scott Morrison and Treasurer Josh Frydenberg, would soon 'snap back'. We had to 'draw the line somewhere'. And that line quickly became painfully clear for those on the wrong side of it. No migrant workers. No public university staff. No international students. No casual workers. Not only did free childcare end after three months (and preschools were excluded from that brief period of respite), but early childhood educators were the first to lose access to the JobKeeper payment. That's right. The first group of workers to lose government assistance was one of the lowest paid, most female-dominated workforces in the country.

JobKeeper was always meant to be temporary. It was an emergency measure, as was the Coronavirus Supplement. A short-term solution to a (hopefully) short-term crisis. But there was no plan for the long term. No across-the-board increase of welfare payments, something that almost every business group, think tank, academic and economist recommended as beneficial to the nation's long-term future.

It was both an extraordinary achievement and a squandered opportunity. For a brief moment in time, Australia fixed homelessness, poverty and removed one of the biggest barriers to women's working lives – unmanageable childcare costs. People living on the streets, unable to access oversubscribed homelessness services, were housed in inner-city hotels to prevent them spreading the virus. Whatever the motivation, for many homeless Australians, it meant a warm bed, decent food and a safe place to live for the first time in years. Who knew it was so easy?

I know these programs cost billions of dollars and there is not an endless supply of government money. But I don't understand why the only option was to get rid of them rather than look for ways to pay for continuing them. There is a strong economic case for all of them. Let's consider each in turn.

In the first four weeks of the pandemic, more than 5000 homeless Australians were taken off the streets and housed in empty hotels and student accommodation. A little over 8000 people were estimated to be sleeping rough in Australia each night before the pandemic, so this was a considerable shift. It was a temporary but hugely beneficial decision for all of us. It prevented the virus spreading through vulnerable people on the streets and from them to the rest of the community, and it gave all those people money to spend on food, clothes and medical care.

Sleeping rough is physically dangerous, impacts mental health and wellbeing and actually costs a lot of money. Bevan Warner from Launch Housing told the ABC that the Covid-19 model of housing the homeless was cheaper than letting people languish on the street. 'It costs more in police call-outs, and having doctors and nurses treat people in emergency wards, than it does to provide people with a home,' Warner said to ABC journalist Ben Knight. 'It's cheaper to get people a home. It'll save money … With the 1000 clients that we have currently in emergency accommodation, we'd be saving $15 million a year.' At the time of writing, no state government has proposed continuing their program of providing free accommodation and services to people experiencing homelessness.

Single older women are the fastest growing group of people experiencing homelessness, with a significant number fleeing violent home situations. The majority of those women don't actually sleep rough but that doesn't make being homeless any less terrifying. Kim* came to Australia when she was nine years old. She's now forty-seven. Her family fled Africa after her father, grandfather and uncle were murdered, as her mother and sisters watched, by men in uniform. She learned to speak English and finished Year Twelve with good marks. She never received any counselling or help to deal with the trauma of her early years and the effects started to show after she left school. One of the ways it manifested was a growing gambling addiction. Unable to understand what was happening to her or how to manage it, she started stealing from the company she worked for.

Kim was arrested, charged and sentenced to seven months in prison. She says now that she's glad she got caught. 'I know what I did was very wrong,' she says. 'It was a relief when I got caught. For so long I was doing this thing and I couldn't stop. When the police came, they stopped me, and I was grateful. I went to prison, which was right. That is what happens to people who do wrong. I was there for seven months, and I vow to myself and my family I will never do such things again. But now I cannot work. No one wants a criminal for their job. I live now in my sister's garage. Her husband does not like it, but she cares for me, and she knows I have nowhere to go, so she makes him let me stay. I don't go into the house very much because it angers him, but I am very grateful to have this bed and safe place. He is a good man. He just know[s] I will be here forever, and he wants to have his family. I keep trying to get jobs, but it is very difficult. No one wants to hire someone like me.'

Tens of thousands of women in their fifties and sixties and older are living like Kim. Some are sleeping in their cars. Others are in converted garages, unused caravans, couches or – if they're lucky – spare rooms. They are at the mercy of the family and friends who house them, sometimes lovingly, sometimes reluctantly, some of them barely able to manage housing costs themselves. For those older women, it's not just the fear of losing their precarious bed, it's also the knowledge that there is nothing they can do to change their situation. In 2001, women over fifty years of age were just under 5 per cent of all unemployment benefit recipients. By 2019, that figure had increased to 20 per cent and one-third of the women over fifty-five receiving the payment had been on it for more than five years. As well as emergency housing for people sleeping rough, we need a huge investment in social housing. Not only would this give safety and security to the older women who cannot get paid work, it would provide a huge economic boost in jobs in the construction sector. Secure housing would also mean older people and people with disabilities would have more money to put back into the economy by spending it on health care, warm clothes, and birthday cakes. Everybody wins.

Childcare delivers considerable benefits for children in the form of early education, particularly for children from economically disadvantaged households. It also allows both parents to return to paid work more easily and is a key driver of gender equality. Currently, childcare costs take 16 per cent of the average Australian family's net income. This compares with 10 per cent internationally. The Parenthood, Australia's leading lobby group for parents, says that free early childhood education and care would cost around $20 billion annually. That's a significant increase on top of current Australian government spending, but the potential benefits are compelling. Modelling by The Grattan Institute suggests it would generate a $27 billion boost to Australia's economic output by increasing the number of women in the workforce. The Parliamentary Budget office estimates that even a 1 per cent reduction in childcare costs increases the hours parents work by 0.25 per cent. The Parenthood's modelling suggests that making childcare free for parents, as it was in the pandemic, would boost women's participation in the workforce to a value of up to $47.2 billion by 2050. All of this without even putting a price on the benefit of early education to the minds of our youngest citizens, including those in vulnerable situations and from disadvantaged backgrounds.

Imagine what could happen if an Australian government had this kind of vision for the future of our economy and particularly for women. Imagine what could have happened if instead of simply saying it costs too much to solve poverty, they recognised that it costs more to perpetuate poverty. Imagine what we could have achieved if we went looking for a way to pay for solutions rather than just abandoning them. There is immeasurable benefit to the kind of policies that lift people out of poverty and prevent others falling into it. Permanently. It seems pie in the sky, despite the compelling economic and social case for change. It seems impossible. Ludicrous. Beyond the budget. And yet we did it. We achieved each of these things during the pandemic and we did so without much debate in our nation's parliaments. Radical change for a fairer nation is possible when we want it enough. The most difficult barrier to overcome is that Australians have become so used to seeing the wealthy rewarded more wealth and the poor punished with more poverty that we've forgotten there could be a better way to run the country.

In 2018, the top 20 per cent of wealth owners in Australia had ninety times the wealth of the lowest 20 per cent. Pause for a moment and let that sink in. That's personal wealth of, on average, $3.3 million, compared to just $36 000. And we know there are people in that top 20 per cent worth a lot more than $3.3 million. Most of those individuals did pretty well in the pandemic. In fact, the combined wealth of Australian billionaires increased by more than 50 per cent in 2020. While the Coronavirus Supplement may have temporarily lifted the most disadvantaged people out of poverty, almost all of it was spent on household bills and groceries. There wasn't a whole lot of buying shares or investing in property development.

Australia has always considered itself the lucky country. Somewhere that anyone could come and have a go, make something of themselves and live a comfortable life. We say we value egalitarianism and fairness. But the realities of our economy suggest otherwise.

When politicians talk about 'the economy', it often sounds like the economy is only about jobs. It isn't. A national economy has many moving parts. International trade, domestic agriculture, climate change, an increasingly bellicose China, roiling global markets, unpredictable fluctuations in the value of the Australian dollar and knock-on effects on export and import markets. All these things interact in complex ways and can have a huge impact on how we live. The economy is also about people. In fact, it is mostly about people. It's about us. You, me, Maria, Alice, and Linh. The people who buy movie tickets and takeaway coffees. The people who check what's on sale before choosing what to buy at the supermarket and go camping at Easter. It's the people who worry about getting their rental bond back or making the next mortgage payment. The people who buy lottery tickets even though they know they'll never win because sometimes it's nice to give into the daydream. It's the women who buy birthday presents they can't afford for their grandkids and survive by couch surfing even though they've never heard the term.

The private, anxious economic questions we ask ourselves all the time about what we should do in our lives are both personal and political. Should I retire now or work a few more years to boost my superannuation? Should I save this cash or take a much-needed holiday? Can the kids go another term without new shoes? Should I spend money on private school or save it for my kid's university studies? Should I go out for dinner or stay home and eat leftovers? Do I borrow money to buy a tiny apartment or keep renting a house and pay someone else's mortgage? Should I take the risk of starting the small business I've always dreamed of or stick with my unfulfilling but secure job? Should I renovate the bathroom or put that money into superannuation? Should I buy a new car or pay extra off the mortgage? Should I go back to work even though my income will barely cover childcare costs? Do I buy Australian-made or just get whatever is cheaper? Can I afford to have another baby? How can I leave him when I have nowhere to go?

The aggregate of all the choices made by millions of people every day are the moving parts of our economy. And they are unpredictable. Which is why economics is part science, part psychology and part guesswork. All of this was true before Covid-19 and those same questions remain. But we have new ones as well. Should I book a holiday interstate or not risk getting stuck on the wrong side of a border closure? When will my mum get vaccinated overseas and does that mean we can see each other again? Should I wear my mask at the supermarket even if it isn't mandatory? Should I be buying toilet paper for the next lockdown? Should I sell my shares in airlines? What happens to me if we go into recession? Will I miss out on a promotion if I keep working from home? Are my parents really safe in an aged care facility? Have I washed my hands enough today? So many questions and with most of them, we will never know the answers until it's too late to change our minds. The mental gymnastics of everyday life during a global pandemic and national recession are so depleting.

Economists say that people make rational decisions based on logical assessment of the facts. Most of us like to believe that we do this, but the truth is almost no one really does. We make decisions based on how we feel, and then we backtrack or cherrypick facts to rationalise our choices. Take my own internal battle about early superannuation access. I *knew* it was not a good idea, but I *felt* like I needed it, so I justified my feelings by telling myself a safe car was more important than retirement savings. Without my mother's intervention, I would have gone with what I felt, not what I knew, and it would not have been a rational or fact-based decision. The decisions we make today matter but we're also at the whim of decision-makers and the myths that influence our feelings even more than the thing we know to be true.

It was only a few years ago I was living in a one-bedroom flat with two teenage children. The flat was above a shop and had no insulation. One very hot summer's day, my then sixteen-year-old daughter got heat stroke from sitting in our lounge room. After that, I had to send her to stay with my mother whenever the temperature got above 35 degrees. We couldn't leave because we were living on just my intermittent income, and I never had enough left over to cover the costs of moving. When you're barely making rent each month, there's just no way to save the full first month's rent and a bond for a better place. Add on all the costs of removalists, utilities connections, carpet cleaning and all the other bits and pieces you have to pay to move to a new house and it quickly becomes impossible. So, my family stayed in our little oven far longer than we should have. God knows what it did to our health and wellbeing. The stress alone was unbearable. We paid a fortune in heating bills during the winter. I would work in cafés and libraries during the summer when working from home became too hot and physically unsafe. We got by.

We managed. But it wasn't comfortable and none of us were at our best at school or work. And we were only there for a couple of years, not a lifetime.

It is expensive to be poor. With no savings, nothing in the bank and no credit card, you shop when you get paid – and even when you spend all of it, you don't have enough so you buy what you need that day. Toilet paper is much cheaper if you buy it in bulk ($15 for thirty-two rolls, or 19 cents per roll), but if you have to manage a weekly budget that has no room for an extra $12 on loo rolls, you simply don't have that option and you buy the two pack for $3 ($1.50 per roll). It costs nearly eight times more to wipe a poor bum than a rich one. Rice is another thing that's much cheaper when bought in bulk. Flour is the same. Most washing detergents are cheaper if you buy those really big packets but sometimes, they're $45 and I can get two meals for that price. This is the stuff well-off people grab off the shelves without even thinking about the price. Even people who are just comfortable can stock up on two-for-one deals or buy-five-and-pay-for-four, accessing the discounts only extended to those who can pay for more. This all sounds trivial until you add it all up and realise that the cost of buying all those things daily instead of monthly can be around $100 a week. Then add the cost of repairing things when they stop working. A cheap washing machine is more likely to break than an expensive one, and then suddenly you're paying laundromat fees and taking time away from paid work to schlep to the laundromat once a week and wait three hours to wash your clothes. Shoes with holes in them become uncomfortable, so you get blisters and sores, bumps and lumps that become orthopaedic problems that are too expensive to fix. The penalties for late payment on overdue bills add up and if it gets so bad that they disconnect you, there's another payment for reconnection. The price for being poor grows bigger every day, and every week you fall further and further behind.

Before the introduction of the Coronavirus Supplement, people on JobSeeker were existing on a base rate of $284 per week. That put everyone in Australia who couldn't get a job below the poverty line. When the supplement was first introduced, it gave those people an extra $275 a week. People on Single Parent Payment, Austudy and Youth Allowance also received the boost. For six months, all of those people were able to eat properly and pay their bills on time. It was a rare chance to get ahead. To buy forty-eight toilet rolls instead of six. To save up and fix the oven so that cooking at home was possible again. To heat the house in winter and cool it in summer. The increased payments meant that our poorest citizens were able to live a basic, but safe and healthy life, something I think most Australians expect we should all have. We all like to believe we'd be looked after if things didn't go our way and we lost work, lost a partner, lost our homes or our security. But outside of the pandemic, the safety net was full of holes – and with the removal of the Coronavirus Supplement – all those holes are back.

Remember that to stay on the payment, you also have to apply for jobs. Lots of them. Including ones that you don't necessarily want. While you might start out with a couple of good outfits to wear to job interviews, what do you do if your weight changes or the clothes tear or something needs to be dry-cleaned and you can't afford it? Haircuts for women are difficult to find for less than $60. Shoes scuff and wear thin. How do you impress a potential employer when you know you don't look good? Your confidence is dented and your sense of self suffers. You've got so many worries about how you'll survive, and you just don't have the headspace to do the work of putting in a great job application or a sparkling interview.

Stay on $284 a week for too long and you can never catch up.

I've largely spoken about the experience of women at a macro level because collectively we shared so much during the pandemic. However, Australian women are not a homogeneous group. I'm white, middle class, inner-city dwelling and slowly coming to grips with the fact that I no longer count as a 'young woman'. My friend Fatima*, who was born in India, worked too long and too hard and expended far too much energy facing down racism and sexism from hospital management and patients throughout the pandemic. Alice, working at a supermarket, kept her job but had to live with ongoing violently racist abuse at the checkout. Maria's cleaning income largely disappeared, and she doesn't know if she'll ever be able to get back to where she was before 2020 or restock her freezer again. I was exhausted by my isolation and the constant worry about what isolation would do to my mother and my son, who both live alone. And, of course, my hopeless hamster wheel of trying to create work where work did not exist. We all had very different experiences of the pandemic, but we all felt wrung-out by fear and worry about the future.

By contrast, another friend of mine, Sally, tells me that 2020 was the best year she's ever had. Sally is a trans woman who couldn't transition until she was in her forties. As almost all trans people do, Sally suffered terrible depression before she was able to live as her true self – and terrible discrimination afterwards. Sally says that 2020 was the first time she felt truly lucky. That's not something she's ever felt before. 'I kept my job. I had a secure place to live. I was doing well, but I knew so many other people who weren't. And I was able to help them. I don't think I've ever gone as long without suffering depression as I did last year. It was an amazing feeling.' She says part of the reason was that she didn't feel as alone in isolation because everyone was isolated. 'Not that I would ever wish it on anyone, but when I have my moments of intense depression, I shut myself off from the world and in lockdown it felt like other people might understand a bit of what I go through.' The other reason Sally felt so much better during 2020 was her job. She works as a security officer at one of Melbourne's major universities. She knows her workmates respect her level of training and abilities, so she feels safe at work. She was also able to take on extra shifts and save money during lockdown. 'I'm debt-free now, for the first time in a long time, so that feels pretty good,' she says. The change in the rental market in Melbourne meant she was able to move from her small flat to a small house with a garden and a garage. Her three passions in life are gardening, vintage Mustang cars and her cats. 'I feel pretty lucky now. It's not something I feel in most of my life. Being a transgender woman is not lucky. No one would choose this. But I am who I am. I'm the same person I always was because I was always Sally. I knew that since before I could talk. I'm not sure if it's happiness, I don't think I've ever really been happy, but I am more content now. I have friends. I have my garden and my garage. Most of the time I'm treated with respect. What more can you ask for?'

Women in precarious circumstances, or women working on the frontline of health care and aged care, had a very different 2020. While healthcare workers didn't necessarily have personal financial hardship, they were much more likely to succumb to the Covid-19 infection itself. Covid-19, where it doesn't kill, has long-lasting physical effects in up to 40 per cent of cases. Almost every study of poverty, particularly long-term poverty, highlights illness and disability as a significant causal factor. Being sick is expensive. So is being disabled. While we tend to focus on the marginalisation and pain of people with chronic illness, we don't talk enough about the economic effects. And again, the effects vary hugely. A doctor in an emergency department who has long-term Covid-19 effects probably has a better chance of working part-time in less demanding roles while she recovers, and of being able to access sick pay in the meantime. A migrant woman working as a nurse's aide might incur the same risk of contracting Covid-19, but she has fewer options to earn income or access paid leave if she does become sick.

When we delve into the diverse and varied circumstances of women both during the pandemic and emerging from it, patterns emerge. Just as doctors and nurses and hospital cleaning staff are more exposed to the disease, some groups of women are more exposed during an economic downturn. Those groups are not defined by income alone either. A woman who owns her own home, has no dependants and has a relatively low income may not be living in poverty. Or at least not in the same way as someone who earns twice as much but is paying high rent and has several young children.

The cost of living is not the same in inner-city Sydney as it is in rural Western Australia. Items that were once considered luxuries, such as air conditioning or broadband, can become expensive necessities for someone who works from home in a poorly insulated flat in Adelaide, where temperatures in summer are regularly over 40 degrees. The pandemic has changed everyone's circumstances to some extent and often in ways that were not predicted or catered for by governments.

The women at the highest risk of poverty are single mothers, Indigenous Australians and women with disabilities. The children of all the women in those groups are also at significantly higher risk of living in poverty. It's not just about getting less food – most mothers will go without to make sure their children are fed – it's about growing up with possibilities. Even in my worst moments of not having enough to live on, I always knew life could be better. I'd done it, seen it, lived it, grew up with it. But how do you convince a child that hard work is all you need when, from infancy, they've watched their mother work incredibly hard without ever earning more than an intermittent minimum wage? Those children learn the unfairness of life too early. They know that hard work doesn't bring its own rewards when the opportunities aren't there to match the effort.

Research by the Productivity Commission in 2018 looked at various forms of 'material deprivation' as a means of measuring poverty. In other words, they were looking at people who cannot afford the basic things we expect Australians to have, such as food, utilities, clothes, medical care and a safe home. The Commission also considered questions such as, could you find $500 in an emergency? Can you pay for hobbies and sporting activities for children? Can you afford to stay warm in winter? Do you have a phone, a washing machine and a fridge? Do you catch up with friends or family at least once a month? People who regularly answer no to three or more of these questions are considered poor. By this definition, single parents – at least 85 per cent of whom are women – experience three times the deprivation of partnered parents. This, as a statistic, sounds a bit cold and distant. I was part of that statistic and living it is anything but distant. Believe me, the reality of that deprivation is right up there, smacking you in the face and shoving you in the back with every breath you take.

And, of course, it's people with disabilities, First Nations people and non-English speaking migrants who have it the worst. I honestly can't count the number of times I've written that caveat into an article. That people in these groups are the most disadvantaged, the most marginalised and experience compounding and intersecting discrimination and inequalities. It never fails to enrage me that the media (and I am part of that) keeps saying it, stating the facts, as if acknowledging them is enough. It isn't. Words are not enough. Not nearly enough. We must actually do something.

Australia is one of the richest nations in the world. There is no excuse for the way we treat our sick, our Indigenous and our new citizens. If we can afford to pour hundreds of millions of dollars into propping up coalmining and giving tax dodges to multinational companies, we can afford to make sure everyone in the country has enough food and somewhere safe to live. It has to be the very least we can do, and it should be to our eternal shame that we're not even doing the very least, let alone doing our very best, to make everyone's life safe.

The extra Covid-19 payments gave single mothers and unemployed people six months of life above the parapet of fear and hunger. It was enough to change their daily existence for the better, but not make a permanent shift from the headspace that poverty creates. Poverty can become a habit. When it first happened to me, I was shocked when bills came in that I couldn't pay, or when food ran out and I couldn't afford more. After two years of it, however, I stopped being shocked. I never stopped being afraid, but I did get used to it. I forgot what it was like to buy a steak because I liked it or a packet of biscuits as a treat. Every cent mattered and I counted them all. Luxuries became unaffordable. After my debit card was knocked back too many times, I'd shop with a pen and paper so that I could add up the total before I got to the register. Handing back tampons and bread to cut $7 off the total bill while shoppers behind me sighed with impatience was not a humiliation that I needed to endure more than once. I have been lucky since then and I don't pay much attention to the running total of my grocery shop anymore. But I'll never forget the days I had to do it. So, I can completely understand the dread when you've been in that position, escaped it, and then see it coming back at you like a freight train full of horror.

Despite the tabloid stereotype, single mothers are not irresponsible teens popping out babies so they can live off the public teat. Most single mothers are women who have escaped unhappy or even abusive relationships and are now caring for children they never anticipated they would be bringing up alone. A 2018 survey by the Council for Single Mothers and their Children found that the average age of single mothers is forty-one and that almost half of them are university educated. Salary, not welfare, is the main source of income for more than half of them. Over 70 per cent have full-time care of their children and about a third never or rarely receive child support from their children's father. In 2018, the unpaid child support debt for payments managed by the Department of Health and Human Services was $1.6 billion, with almost no effort made by the department to collect on those debts. It goes without saying: this money that fathers refuse to pay towards caring for their kids would make an enormous difference to the lives of women and children.

Lockdowns were tough on relationships, but we don't yet know for sure how many actually ended. Data shows that domestic abuse increased during lockdown and many women experienced family violence for the first time. The dynamics of family violence are complex. It's not impossible that a man who was not in any way abusive or controlling prior to lockdown could become so under the pressure of isolation and job losses. But it's more likely that there was some level of existing abuse going on in those households that may not previously have manifested as physical violence. Those women have experienced trauma. At the very least, if they leave their abusive partners, they will likely suffer damage to their confidence and ability to push forward into the demanding life of paid work and single parenting. For the women who don't choose to separate, even if the physical violence de-escalates, fear and loneliness created by the abuse can hurt their health, confidence and their ability to rebuild life on their own terms.

Kate* married Henry* when she was twenty-two years old. She left him sixteen years later, just after her thirty-eighth birthday. In their time together, Henry inflicted multiple fractures and so many punches to the head that Kate has an acquired brain injury. She has trouble explaining exactly how this affects her, but she can describe some of the symptoms. 'I get these headaches, just out of nowhere, like I've been bashed again,' Kate explains. 'I'm supposed to take [painkillers] for it but sometimes I can't find them. I can't remember where I put them. I can't remember things a lot. I get so mad because I think I used to remember better and it's so … so …' At this point, Kate curled her hands into fists and started to cry. The word she was searching for and couldn't find was 'frustrating'. Kate has trouble controlling her emotions, she struggles with short-term memory, and she can't complete routine tasks reliably. She wants to work. Apart from needing the money, she likes having a structure to her life and regular contact with people. She's tried many times to get a job, sometimes successfully, but because of her brain injury and the damage to her ankles and wrists, her jobs never last very long. She struggles to comprehend Centrelink's many requirements and has spent the last few years bouncing between paid work, unemployment benefits and the Disability Allowance. Several times in the last ten years, Kate has lost her welfare payments due to her inability to understand and comply with Centrelink's bureaucratic demands. Her injuries will not heal any more than they have and now that she's in her late forties, it's unlikely she will ever find long-term paid work.

During the Melbourne lockdown, Kate received the Coronavirus Supplement, and she didn't have to worry about reporting all her failed job applications to Centrelink. She spent the extra money on warm clothes, an electric blanket, and weekly online sessions with a therapist. I checked in with her in March 2021. Kate told me that almost an entire year of regular therapy, which she had never been able to do before, made an enormous difference to her fear and anger. She also said she was terrified about the end of the Coronavirus Supplement and the creation of the 'JobDobber' hotline, a new initiative where employers can report anyone on JobSeeker who refuses a job or performs badly in an interview. As much as Kate wants to work, there are some things she has to avoid because the effects of Henry's violence are still with her. Dealing with abusive customers makes working in retail difficult. Angry or derogatory comments from harsh supervisors can send Kate into a panic attack. Too much noise and confusion can overwhelm her, sometimes even sparking migraines. Kate is still looking for a job, but she can only say yes to the *right* job. She doesn't know – and nor does anyone else – whether this will be deemed an acceptable reason to turn down a job offer if someone reports her to JobDobber.

The economic cost of men's violence against women is high. A 2015 study by PricewaterhouseCoopers suggested it could be as much as $22 billion a year in 'lost productivity, reduced consumption and premature mortality', as well as medical, legal, and administration costs – all dry economic terms for lives that have been shredded by men's violence.

Hearing all this could well be enough to make any woman think twice if she's considering leaving a violent relationship.

It's difficult enough if the relationship is just unhappy, but if it's abusive or dangerous, the fear is exponentially higher and the outcome even worse. These issues are deeply personal for the women living through them, but the solutions are structural. Governments must stop ignoring women in crisis.

Those crises don't always have a clear beginning. They don't even necessarily involve violence and trauma. They can start with what seems like a reasonable choice, such as deciding to leave paid work for a few years to look after children. But the longer women are out of the full-time workforce, the less money they earn when they return. When a woman does return, she often goes back to work part-time and, in reality, may well reduce her hours and pay but be slugged with the same workload. Working mothers' career progression often slows down and so the cost of childcare compared to their potential income becomes a poorer equation. Again, the cost of childcare is only ever deducted from women's income, not the family income or potential future income. I understand it, because the long-term benefits of gaining skills and experience by staying in a job don't always stack up against the exhaustion of trying to manage full-time paid work and full-time unpaid care work at home. The effect can be that women who have not consistently worked full-time are perceived as less valuable employees, so they're paid less and not promoted as often. Meanwhile, their partners, the much lauded 'hardworking family men', are solidifying their claim as the experienced, reliable breadwinners. The more reliant a woman becomes on a male partner, the more vulnerable she is to coercion or financial abuse, which can spiral into physical violence. The pandemic made women's economic and personal circumstances exponentially more dangerous. Cashing in on previously saved superannuation or dropping out of the workforce to homeschool may have seemed like smart choices at the time because the immediate is always more urgent. But in the future, these choices – family choices – will hurt women most. Some small decisions taken today will culminate into intractable poverty decades after the fact.

Women with children are especially vulnerable because of the additional responsibilities they face and the added pressures to stay in abusive relationships. The risk of violence, of divorce and of poverty in old age are yet more reasons all parents need jobs that accommodate raising children and working outside the traditional nine-to-five, Monday to Friday office job. We must stop forcing women to choose between paid work and parenting. Mothers *and* fathers need affordable, quality childcare that caters for non-standard hours. All parents would benefit if we encouraged the continuation of the flexible working arrangements that we had under Covid-19 rather than try to drag everything back to the pre-Covid status quo. And we must stop talking and thinking about childcare as a women's issue and cost. Mothers should not carry the weight of parenting alone.

Men are parents too. We started to make that change during the pandemic, with free childcare (albeit briefly), flexible work and men becoming more involved in caring for their children. If we can hold on to those changes and improve on them, everyone wins. Doing nothing is also a choice and we don't have to decide to do nothing about making life better and safer for women.

The Coronavirus Supplement lifted more than 600 000 Australians out of poverty. Temporarily. Yes, we do have a huge national debt, but the money borrowed for JobKeeper happened at a time when the Australian economy had virtually screamed to a halt. Giving money to poor people boosts economic growth far more than giving money to rich people. Poor people spend every dollar they have and they're much more likely to spend it locally. Rich people save, they invest in shares which might send profit overseas and are more likely to buy imported luxury goods. The Productivity Commission, the Business Council of Australia, Chartered Accountants Australia and New Zealand, the Governor of the Reserve Bank and Financial Counselling Australia have all called for large and permanent increases to unemployment benefits. It's worth noting that none of these are groups known for their left-leaning economic views. There is a clear and strong economic case for boosting JobSeeker on an ongoing basis, not only to keep Australians out of poverty but to bolster economic activity as a whole.

We learned a lot in 2020 but the price was too high. Too many people died. Too many people suffered. Too many people are still living with the effects of grief, business failures, job losses and isolation. It shouldn't have taken a global pandemic to show us that we can provide free childcare and turn it around in about a week. Or that we can solve Australia's homelessness problem. Or finally recognise that the workers in the lowest paid and most insecure jobs are the ones we depend on the most.

We also discovered that there is a clear path to ending poverty. That's right – actually ending poverty. As Glyn Davis, CEO of Paul Ramsay Foundation, told the Future Women podcast: 'if you were among the poorest of Australians, it's possible that 2020 was your best year ever.' When I told my friend Julie* about this last week, she burst into tears. Julie is a single mother of two small children and her life was changed by the Coronavirus Supplement. I thought she was crying with relief at feeling heard and understood. I was wrong. Julie was crying because she felt guilty. 'People were dying. *Dying*. People in old age homes were dying all alone and their families couldn't even have funerals for them,' she said. 'And I spent six months being a terrible, terrible person because I haven't been that happy or relaxed for years. I paid my rent. I was ahead on all my bills and the cupboards were full. It took so many people dying to make that happen. I still can't get over how dreadful I feel that I was so relieved.'

When Australia's nationwide lockdown sent hundreds of thousands of workers out of the office to work from home, we discovered a new divide. The old classifications of class still have some relevance but they're not really accurate anymore. We used to talk about white-collar and blue-collar workers. During Covid-19, that changed to talking about flexible workers and essential workers. Doctors, delivery drivers, security guards, nurses, supermarket workers, emergency services, and cleaners do not have the option to work from home. Nor can we survive very long without them. Hairdressers, personal care workers, hospitality staff and childcare workers also can't work from home, but we can survive without them if we have to, although our lives are poorer for it. In the past, lawyers, public servants, accountants, insurance adjusters, call centre staff and, yes, journalists too, had all been told that our presence in the office was mandatory. Then, suddenly, we discovered that just wasn't true. Our working lives changed profoundly as we became at-home workers, blending our personal and professional lives in ways we'd never imagined possible before.

Covid-19 was a great leveller. Distinctions of class did not mean high-earning Australians could embrace at-home work because of their status. Essential workers were essential, regardless of income. Both surgeons and supermarket checkout operators were required to risk their health by continued contact with the public.

Working from home has many advantages. I should know – I've been doing it for over a decade. It's often the small things that add up to better quality of life. I can get laundry done in five-minute stints while I'm working. A lunchbreak can incorporate a trip to the shops a few times a week rather than wasting hours on the weekend doing a full grocery run. I can think my way through a problem while vacuuming the living room. I have even been known to make a curry while dictating notes to my phone. I don't have time or money eaten away by a long commute or the ridiculous time wasted on hair, make-up and office clothing. I can, and frequently do, work in my pyjamas. The sum total of all these small advantages during the week often means all my domestic work is done by the weekend. I have more time to be with people I love, to have fun and genuinely enjoy a restorative two days rather than being tied to the domestic grind. The downside, of course, is isolation. Working from home can be lonely, and there is a blurring of lines between working and switching off. These are not small things but there are ways to manage them. I find the trade-off is well worth it.

Many people who were able to work from home during 2020 found that life gets easier with flexible work. The Victorian Equal Opportunity and Human Rights Commission conducted a survey of just over 1500 Victorian workers who are parents, carers or have a disability. An overwhelming 85 per cent said they wanted to continue with flexible work after the pandemic is over, and almost half said that flexible arrangements made them more productive at work. It's so goddam simple now. We don't have to do anything extra to make flexible work happen because we've already done it. Australia sent an entire workforce home for months and it was fine. Employers adapted their practices. Meetings moved online. We learned to pick up the phone more often and more meaningfully. Employees changed the set-up of their houses. Found space where they could work. Got comfortable and toasted good riddance to the daily commute. For many of us, it was better than fine. The challenge now is adopting a power pose, smiling and making soothing noises while we tell our bosses that we're not going back to the way things were. The world has changed, and we don't need to wind it back just because HR departments are scared of something new and mayoral offices are screaming about losing car-parking revenue.

Helen* is a woman in her thirties who works in insurance. Helen had been on the verge of giving up work before lockdown. 'It was just getting too hard,' she told me. 'Getting one kid to childcare, the other one to school, and myself to work, then having to collect everyone and get us all home, fed, bathed and into bed. Honestly, I was so tired and strung-out. It was too much.' Helen said that she changed her mind after lockdown forced her employer to accept the team would be working from home. It was something she had never thought possible before the pandemic. 'I love my job and I love working,' she said. 'I never really wanted to give it up. When we started working from home, it was like a life raft landed on my life and made everything okay.' Helen's employer has agreed that she can continue working from home at least three days a week now that Covid-19 restrictions have ended. 'It's awful to be glad about something so terrible,' she says. 'But that pandemic saved my career. There's no way they would have agreed to this before lockdown.'

Akachi* works as a public servant. She told me that her home life was easier during lockdown and her work life also became safer. 'My boss isn't really abusive,' Akachi says carefully. 'But he hangs over me all the time and makes these little comments, putting me down. It's not outright anger, just little sneers and eye rolls when I ask questions or make suggestions.' Working in this environment made Akachi think that she wasn't very good at her job but that changed when she started working at home. 'I'd still speak to him [my boss] every day, but it was different,' she tells me. 'We'd still talk about what I was going to do each day, but it was on a Zoom call in front of everyone and he couldn't get away with those kinds of sneers when everyone was watching. So I'd just do my update then turn Zoom off and get my work done.' It took a few weeks, but Akachi started to realise that, actually, she's very good at her job. 'I get everything done on time and it's good work,' she says defiantly. 'I'm much happier working from home and I've already said I want to keep doing it.'

And then there is Marta*, a twenty-eight-year-old lawyer, who told me that she'd been on the verge of quitting her job due to sexual harassment. 'It was nothing physical, not even always verbal,' she explained. 'But you know that thing gross men do when they're looking you up and down? Or he'd stare at my boobs or my bum, that kind of thing that is just creepy and gross but how do you make a complaint about someone looking at you?' Marta says that working from home brought the sexual harassment to an abrupt end. 'I recorded all the Zooms,' she says. 'I told him it was because then I didn't have to take notes and could concentrate on the conversations. He couldn't really object, and he knew better than to try anything while I was recording it, so there's none of that stuff anymore. I can just concentrate on getting my work done. I don't have to be scared of working late or who else is in the office at lunchtime. I feel like a completely different person. There's no way I'm going to go back to working in an office again.'

Clinical terms like 'sexual harassment in the workplace' can obscure the reality of the creepy, frightening, and degrading abuse that does real harm to women who are just trying to do their job. In the majority of cases, it's done to women by a man who has the power to take away their job, career and income and never suffer any consequences. The effects are not small. It can push some women out of the workforce completely. Others are left with their confidence shredded and their faith in their future destroyed. It's both horribly shocking and horribly unsurprising that it happens so often and is reported so rarely.

The Australian Human Rights Commission's 'Respect@Work' report sat untouched in a drawer in former Attorney-General Christian Porter's office for over a year. It shouldn't have. It was an incredibly incisive and damning report, and it proposed a number of effective solutions. The report found just under 40 per cent of Australian women who had been in the workforce in the previous five years had experienced sexual harassment at work. Among the 18–29 age group, this figure went up to 53 per cent.[12] More than half of our promising young women damaged like this at the very beginning of their careers. It's iniquitous. And those figures are an absolute minimum because there will inevitably have been people who were too traumatised to take the survey, or not ready to talk about what was done to them.

Some of the recommendations in the Respect@Work report are so simple it defies belief that they even need to be said, such as making it a positive duty for employers to take reasonable action to eliminate sexual discrimination and harassment. In the same way we would never accept an employer waiting for someone to fall through an unsafe floor before fixing it, why would we accept that someone must suffer (and prove) sexual abuse at work before their employer acts to prevent it? Why is it acceptable that some employers (such as government ministers) are exempt? Or that sexually harassing someone is not immediate grounds for firing someone?

Of course, not everyone is safer at home than work. For women who live with abusive men, lockdown was truly terrifying. Much of my journalism is about men's violence, and it's not uncommon for women to contact me with their stories. One woman, let's call her Anne, was happy for me to share her email here. Anne wrote: 'It wasn't just that I couldn't get away from him. It was that he knew no one else was going to see me. There was no one to ask if I was okay or where the bruises came from … He didn't have to be careful anymore. The tension kept getting higher and higher. I couldn't sleep. I couldn't think. I definitely couldn't work.' Things only changed for Anne when she and her colleagues were allowed to return to the office. 'I think I was about to get fired because I'd been so useless working from home,' she says. 'My boss is pretty great though. After I told her what had been happening, she called a helpline for me and gave me heaps of time off so I could move out and clear my head. I had to go to part-time, because I just wasn't able to work full-time anymore. But at least I have a job and I can get more hours when I'm ready.'

Along with the sad and distressing stories, there were also some lovely anecdotes that came from most of the country being sent home to work. Jamila Rizvi, who edited this book, told me that she and her husband would walk together to pick up their five-year-old son from school. And then they'd all walk home together as a family. She told me this was 'just not something that would have ever happened before lockdown. Normally my husband and I would have been rushing home from the CBD, texting frantically about who was doing the pick-up and how on earth we'd get dinner cooked so our son would have a decent bedtime. The slightly slower pace and the possibility of working together to raise our son rather than working in shifts has been properly delightful.'

Another friend of mine, Danya*, told me that her husband has taken enthusiastically to vacuuming, something she would never have expected before the forced time inside. 'He says he finds it really satisfying,' Danya says, bewildered. 'I don't get it, but frankly he's always been a bit of a weirdo and I'm not going to fight him for it. You wouldn't believe how clean our floors are now.' Another friend, Annika*, tells me that working from home is fine. 'I mean, I can take it or leave it, but I definitely didn't do as much day drinking when I worked at the office,' she jokes. I overheard a few snippets of conversation at the local dog park during Melbourne's long lockdown in 2020. I wrote them down because they summed up so much of what happened in my city during that long, dark winter: 'I've been married to him for fifteen years – how did I not know he's this goddamn annoying?' 'I had to delete Facebook. All those people I used to like have turned into a pack of screaming arseholes. Is that a side effect of Covid?' 'I can't remember, did I actually really want children?' And my personal favourite: 'Welp, that's it for me and bras.'

These are all women on the lucky side of the digital divide. For them, lockdown opened up a world of flexible working arrangements that have made their working lives easier, safer and less expensive. But what about the women on the other side of the divide? During the worst of the pandemic, when I watched the news and another outbreak had been reported, there would be footage of people in hazmat suits walking into the infection site with industrial disinfectant. The people in those suits were almost always women of colour. So many of the essential workers who proved critical to our safety during the pandemic are permanent migrants or working on temporary or student visas. They are aged care workers, industrial cleaners, quarantine security guards, and delivery drivers. These are not the best paid workers; indeed, some of them may be the worst paid. But they are also, as we all discovered, among the most necessary. Certain categories of visa holders have no access to Medicare, childcare benefits or free schooling. They tend to work on casual contracts and aren't entitled to sick leave or carer's leave. Their jobs can – and did – vanish without notice or explanation, and they were not eligible for JobSeeker or JobKeeper. Australia asks them to accept all this insecurity in return for doing the essential work that keeps us safe, healthy, and, during the pandemic, alive. And they do it.

Priya* came to Australia three years ago to study nursing. She was working in the aged care sector before Covid-19 upended all our lives. 'I love my job and my studies,' Priya says. 'I am here because my family gave up so much to send me here. I am never grateful enough for what they did, my parents and grandparents.' Priya feels indebted to her family for the sacrifices they made for her education and opportunities. 'I couldn't ask them for more,' she explains. 'I was working at three different places before the virus. It was the only way I could pay my rent and health insurance and school fees. I did get sick for a while, but I never take time off when I'm sick. If I don't go to work, I can't pay for anything.' When Covid-19 exposed the vulnerabilities of people living in aged care facilities, Priya knew she had to change – even if it cost her money. 'When I realised I could make my patients sick, I knew I had to stay home. It was so scary. I felt so sick and awful. I couldn't stop worrying. What if I lost my job? What if they cancel my visa? I can't explain what it was like. It was the worst thing I've ever gone through.' Priya is hopeful that she will be able to apply for citizenship when she's completed the last few units of her nursing degree. She wants to keep working in aged care. 'It would be much easier if they paid properly, but I'll keep doing it if I can,' she says honestly. 'I love my patients and I really love the work. I just wish they'd change it so we could do the job properly.'

The problems in the aged care sector are extensive and would take an entire book to cover adequately, but Priya's experience is typical of people who work in the sector. She is just one of many migrant workers who do essential work Australians don't want to do, and receives little job security, pay or appreciation in return. Priya's situation also demonstrates how Covid-19 spread so rapidly around the aged care facilities in Victoria – most workers had multiple jobs because the pay in aged care is so poor. Unable to make a living off one job, and unable to even comprehend taking time off if they got sick, those workers felt they had no choice but to keep going to work. Let's hope at least one lesson we learn from Covid-19 is that our essential workers are not just expenses we can cut to increase profit. Treating people with contempt will, eventually, bite you on the arse.

The Victorian government, which had its arse well and truly bitten in 2020, recognised the dangers of insecure work and introduced a pilot scheme in November 2020 to provide sick and carer's pay to casual workers in priority industries. Premier Daniel Andrews said in a press release, 'When people have nothing to fall back on, they make a choice between the safety of their workmates and feeding their family. The ultimate decision they make isn't wrong – what's wrong is they're forced to make it at all.' Again, it should not have taken a pandemic for us to realise how wicked this is, but we can hope businesses now see the value in giving workers respect, adequate pay and decent conditions. If they don't, the same issues will bite the same arses in the next crisis.

I hate feeling pessimistic, but it comes too easily now. I used to be much more optimistic. Maybe I've been changed by too many years of writing about men's violence against women and the poverty that too often awaits women after a lifetime caring for others. Or perhaps I simply now know more about the realities of the world than I used to. Whatever the cause, sometimes I find it difficult to hold on to hope. There are things that help, of course. The disbelieving snort from my daughter when I told her that less than two hundred years ago Australian women were not allowed to vote or own property. The look in comedian Hannah Gadsby's eyes when she stared down the camera lens in the Netflix special *Nanette* and said, 'there is nothing stronger than a broken woman who has rebuilt herself'. Watching Lidia Thorpe and Linda Burney storm into the Federal Parliament and have no time for its bullshit. Seeing singer and legend Dolly Parton contribute funds towards a Covid-19 vaccine and then wear a sexy cold-shoulder top while getting a literal dose of her own medicine. Author Roxane Gay doing pretty much anything. I cannot look at these women, both here in Australia and around the world, and give up on hope.

I also have to keep reminding myself that change is a long game. Hope doesn't come from looking at where we were a week ago or even a year ago. It comes from looking further back and seeing what we have done over decades. I want to see more change in my working lifetime – and I need more years to see that change, to *be* that change. I want to still be writing articles in my old age. I want those articles to be published not despite but *because* of my old age. I want to not have to be writing toothless acknowledgements of the greater danger for women of colour and women with disabilities, not because we've stopped acknowledging it, but because we've eliminated those dangers.

Women changed the world in just one hundred years. It's not perfect yet but we're not finished yet. Just as Covid-19 is not over for anyone until it is over for everyone, no women are free of sexism and racism until all women are free of it. The March4Justice, hastily and raggedly organised in only a couple of weeks, brought nearly 100 000 women out of their homes, workplaces, schools, and universities in March of 2021. Despite all the claims on their time and emotions, women showed up to express their rage, exhaustion and frustration at the violence and injustice that never seems to end. That burst of emotion will subside with time. It has to. Nobody can maintain that level of passion for too long without burning out. But that doesn't mean the emotion will disappear into nothing. Rather, it will harden into determination. Hopefully, that determination will be enough to change all the forces that make women unsafe in their homes and their jobs and their old age.

2020 showed us that childcare and aged care workers, cleaners, shelf stackers and community workers are essential. We must never forget what essential really means. It means we can't do without those workers – we literally can't live without them. We need to recognise women's work. We need to value it properly. And we need to pay women what they're damn well worth. The pandemic also pulled into stark focus the fact that mothers are not the only parents of children. So are non-binary people and trans people – and so are fathers. Men cannot continue to duck responsibility for parenting by claiming 'breadwinner' status and then refuse to acknowledge all the unpaid work women do to make their breadwinning possible. Pay mothers what they're damn well worth or, at the very least, make it possible for them to earn what they're damn well worth.

All the gendered myths about men being better leaders and women being better carers and no other genders being relevant are bullshit. Adhering to them narrows everyone's lives and possibilities. We need to smash them into the ground, leave the wreckage behind, and give everyone the chance to do the best damn work they can do. In the wake of 2020, we must reverse the punitive policy approach to poverty, colonialism, domestic and family abuse, single mothers and homelessness. These are people, not demographics or categories in a statistical report. People. The very best we can do to give people dignity and safety is surely the very least we can do.

I want Alice to go back to work in the supermarket and not have to be afraid of her customers. I want Kate to recover from her trauma and find work that shows her she can be useful, happy and safe. I want Maria to make lasagne for her son because she loves to do it, not because she's afraid he won't have enough to eat if she doesn't. I want Sally to be able to feel happy, even lucky, and not be surprised that she can. I want Priya to keep caring for her patients without appalling working conditions putting her and them in danger. I want my mother to get her vaccine and not have to worry about my financial future. I want my children to have a life of opportunities that are never constrained by their gender. I want everyone to have this because that's the only way any of us have it. I want to believe this is not hopeless idealism but a reality that is reachable and possible in my lifetime.

Pushing back against all the structures that prevent us making these changes will take time, effort and unwavering determination.

I believe we are up to the challenge.

Love.

Santilla Chingaipe

Santilla Chingaipe is a Zambian-born, award-winning journalist and documentary filmmaker. She spent nearly a decade working for SBS World News, which saw her report from across Africa and interview some of the continent's most prominent leaders. Santilla writes regularly for *The Saturday Paper*, and her work explores contemporary migration, cultural identities and politics.

In the early days of the pandemic, I experienced an outpouring of love. My schedule was full of virtual social activities with family and friends near and far. Friday night Zoom cocktails, virtual museum tours, Instagram DJ gigs, weekday workouts, everything in between. We didn't have information about how long Covid-19 would last and we were making a conscious effort to stay connected while awaiting the return of normality. But as the pandemic wore on and the weeks turned into months with no clear end in sight, the novelty of virtual drinks wore off and our phones grew quiet. I felt alone. Trapped in a perpetual Groundhog Day. I think we all did, didn't we? Maybe we had too much time by ourselves, alone with ourselves, with nothing to entertain us but our own thoughts. Would this perpetual state of monotony impact our capacity to love, in all its permutations, and care for one another when so much of our energy was spent on just getting by? How do our relationships change and thrive and endure when we're all preoccupied with our own survival?

Being alone, at home, day in, day out, getting to know the various shades of white on my walls better than I'd ever expected, I thought about love. How love behaves in a crisis. What love feels like from afar. Whether love can get us through all of this. It made me think of something the late, great Maya Angelou said in an interview. She talked about how love can travel and that this is perhaps its greatest power: 'Love says, "I love you. I would like to be near you. I'd like to have your arms around me. I'd like to hear your voice in my ear. But that's not possible now, so I love you."'[13] Right in the middle of lockdown, I could no longer find any truth in Dr Angelou's words. I felt that perhaps any declarations of 'I love you' that were meant for me couldn't find me, alone where I was. Which was on my couch, staring at the ceiling for hours at a time, paralysed by fear and lying in a foetal position. I spent weeks crying myself to sleep from the anxiety and grief of living through a global pandemic. I was mourning the loss of life and of things I'd previously taken for granted. Things like leaving the house, seeing people, and feeling that love.

I had to give up on the plans I'd had for my life, or at least that's how it felt. I questioned my life choices. A career in the arts suddenly seemed indefensibly indulgent when other people were risking their lives on the frontline to keep us all safe. I'm a hopeful person by nature but for the first time I failed to see how things could possibly get better. I usually start my days with a mini dance party in the kitchen while I make my morning coffee. It was a little ritual of joy before the day began and I loved it. That stopped in March of 2020. I couldn't find the right soundtrack for a pandemic. I couldn't stand the sound of anything happy, so I turned the radio off. When I did listen, it was depressingly sad and sombre music. I had trouble articulating my emotions, which is unusual for me. The mantras I normally turned to in sadness and uncertainty weren't enough to lift me out of the fugue state. 'This too shall pass' doesn't quite work in what seems like a never-ending global crisis.

Not knowing how to make sense of this stuff myself, I started googling why I felt so grim; why we all felt so grim. As ever, professionally wise people had something to say. Speaking to the *New York Times* in April 2020, self-help guru Brené Brown suggested that 'a crisis highlights all of our fault lines' and encouraged people to use the time in lockdown for self-reflection. 'We can pretend that we have nothing to learn, or we can take this opportunity to own the truth and make a better future for ourselves and others,' she said.[14] In *The Guardian* in August 2020, writer and lawyer Nyadol Nyuon made a similar argument. 'The plague is not a beautiful thing but something can be retrieved even from the worst of circumstances,' she wrote. 'How we respond to this new reality will be determined by the individual circumstances of our lives and the privileges we enjoy.'[15]

How will we respond to this 'new' reality? It's hard to imagine a return to the pre-Rona times, and yet it's human nature to revert to what's familiar. We need the courage to imagine a new way forward, one that is equitable. But how do we find that courage? Being able to articulate it would be a start.

On an intellectual level, this all made sense – and that helped, a little – but it still didn't explain the listlessness that was brought on by the monotony of isolation. If you turned on the news at any point last year, you'd have heard the word 'unprecedented'. I would place a pretty hefty bet on some dictionary or another making it the word of the year. Apart from being an overused adjective, it also wasn't quite accurate. According to Greek mythology, there is a word for the state of emotions we were feeling: *acedia.*[16] John Cassian, a monk and theologian, wrote in the early fifth century that when a person experiences acedia, they feel 'such bodily listlessness and yawning hunger as though they were worn by a long journey or a prolonged fast.' Cassian further describes a man who 'glances about and sighs that no one is coming to see him. Constantly in and out of his cell, he looks at the sun as if it were too slow in setting.' That all made sense to me.

Moving on a little from the fifth century, psychologist Adam Grant described a similar feeling in April 2021. He called it 'languishing', which describes the sort of joyless aimlessness that has continued for so many Australians in our stop-start emergence from the pandemic. In the *New York Times*, Grant described it as 'a sense of stagnation and emptiness. It feels as if you're muddling through your days, looking at your life through a foggy windshield.'[17] Grant called it the dominant emotion of 2021. Beyond the initial fear and pandemic, the depths of anger and despair, there is a well of nothingness. An emotion that is not quite anxiety, not quite depression but a sort of void.

I was comfortable, safe and had many luxuries during the course of the pandemic that millions of people around the world didn't have access to. Nonetheless, I just didn't care about any of it. Being able to give language to the emotional state brought on by the monotony of life in lockdown made me feel like I wasn't alone in this experience. Knowing that it continued for many people long after Australia was initially considered Covid-free in the dawning days of February 2021 and our borders firmly closed made me feel less alone. While I was apart from those that I love and care about, turning on the television news or flicking through social media gave me an insight into how we were all navigating this pandemic. It helped ease the anxiety and fear because everyone was feeling it – in some way – in every corner of the world. And giving these feelings language, much like when you get to the root of an issue in a therapy session, felt like an 'aha' moment. The language made me feel less alone, even though intellectually I knew I wasn't. Being able to define this experience reminded me that, while physically distanced, we were all in this together. This was a global event, where no person in the world went truly untouched. There was a feeling of community wound up in that togetherness, that collective experience. Even though, of course, we were all being impacted by the pandemic differently.

The pandemic might feel like it's the worst thing to happen to humanity and if hyperbole soothes you then by all means, it is yours. But in reality, it's not. Humanity has been through rather a lot of pandemic-like seismic shifts as a species. Take the Australian context. First Nations communities have known all too well the devastating impact of plagues as a result of colonisation. When European settlers arrived on this continent, they brought with them death, dispossession and disease. According to historical documents,[18] fifteen months after the arrival of the First Fleet in New South Wales, a smallpox epidemic broke out in the colony, leading to devastating consequences for Aboriginal communities, who'd never been exposed to the disease. It is estimated that up to 70 per cent of the Indigenous population died from exposure to the virus. 'There are accounts of people being stacked up in caves,' says Professor Jakelin Troy, a Ngarigu woman from the Snowy Mountains and director of Aboriginal and Torres Strait Islander Research at the University of Sydney. She explains that the elderly, pregnant women, and children were the most susceptible,[19] as always. More diseases like influenza, measles and tuberculosis were introduced next, which also led to fatalities among the Aboriginal population and would go on to have an impact on entire generations. Some of the preventative methods employed during Covid-19, like self-isolation, were also used by Aboriginal people to limit the spread of disease. Professor Troy says that 'Aboriginal people in Sydney were able to manage as far as they could and people kept themselves isolated. There's evidence of people who had the illness camping by themselves and people would bring them food, but they would stay away from them.'

Professor Troy tells me that Indigenous women played a pivotal role in the frontlines during those years. 'It's interesting that when this plague went through, women understood that if you touched somebody, you could get this [disease]. They understood causality in illness and women are often the healers, the midwives.' This cultural act of love was all too evident centuries later when Aboriginal and Torres Strait Islander communities came together to curb the spread of Covid-19. After a long history of neglect and discrimination that led to poor health outcomes, Indigenous Australians took matters into their own hands. The disease was fought locally, with measures led by the Aboriginal Community Controlled Health Service. And they were highly successful. Finding their own solutions ensured First

Nations people, normally highly vulnerable to disease, were able to shield their communities from the virus and record infection rates lower than the rest of the population. It was an important reminder to governments, national and state, that Aboriginal control of Aboriginal affairs can bring about policy outcomes bureaucrats and politicians never could. But it should go beyond being a reminder – as I write this, there have been seven Aboriginal deaths in custody since the start of 2021. And nearly 500 since the Royal Commission in 1991. Most of us know that Indigenous Australians come off worse on every development and health measure that exists. Little is being done to address this. In the aftermath of the pandemic, we must rouse ourselves from this state of acedia to collectively support Indigenous self-representation. Until we centre justice for First Nations people, we cannot fairly describe ourselves as a country which prioritises love and respect among its citizens.

During a state-sanctioned daily walk, I wondered if my experience of lockdown might have been different had I lived with the people I love. I concluded that people who live alone didn't necessarily have it any worse or better than people who were surrounded by family and friends. It was just altogether a different experience.

Single people are almost always forgotten in policy conversations. It was months into the lockdown in Melbourne before officials allowed single people without intimate partners the opportunity to spend time with a friend.[20] Once this was finally allowed, I was so used to being forgotten that I never even bothered to nominate a friend. A few single friends did welcome the change. They said so in our group chat. 'I'm all for being a homebody, but just not even having the choice of being able to have a single person over when you live alone has been very hard,' texted Mia. I responded with '💯'. 'It's such an insult to single people. There's way too much of life geared towards people who are coupled up. It's so much more expensive to be single. Then to add insult to injury, rooting any rando off the street is fine but to have a "bubble" with others who live alone isn't,' said Alice.

According to the most recent ABS data,[21] about half a million Victorians live alone. Across the country, it's around 10 per cent of Australians. One in four households is a single person. That means a quarter of Aussie households have no one to scold for stacking the dishwasher wrong, anyone to yell at them that their TV show is back on after the ads, or anyone to put the kettle on when they're sad. Unsurprisingly, women make up the largest cohort, at 55 per cent, with the median age of women living alone being sixty-four years old, compared to fifty-four for men.[22] Financial considerations aside, it will be interesting to see how so much time spent thinking about our living situations might affect those stats. Maybe more people will couple up, having felt that lockdown loneliness too keenly. Maybe couples and families and flatmates will decide to go out on their own, having spent so much intense time cooped up with the same people. Whether we end up with fewer single-people households, or more, policymakers cannot continue to overlook such a significant portion of the population. The needs of single people are different and meaningful, and they have to be addressed. During a crisis, yes. But also while we're building whatever Australia's new normal will be.

Friendships for single people take on added meaning – in the absence of an intimate partner, we turn to, and rely on, our friends. The pandemic took away the connections with people I wasn't particularly close to but would, on occasion, socialise with. Like the friends who I go dancing with, but rarely catch up with in daylight, or the friends that I meet for classical music concerts and have little else in common. I had one friend who I'd periodically catch up with to play pool at our local pub and as soon as that activity was cancelled, so too was our friendship. Many of these connections were centred around things to do and places to see. I missed what these friendships added to my life, even though the degree of closeness varied. And so I turned to my neighbours who, until that point in my life, I'd largely ignored. I made a conscious effort to get to know people in my building, and soon formed relationships that centred around activities within our immediate community. I wonder if maybe those neighbours were also looking for connection without necessarily articulating it to themselves. The relationships became fundamental to our quiet daily activities. We'd check in on each other and I know that community consciousness will last beyond the pandemic.

Being in prolonged lockdown made me interrogate my intimate relationships and what I wanted out of them. While I'm not sure how I will ever believe in romance again, living through a pandemic really lifted the rose-coloured glasses on what and who I want to spend my time with. I've been known to date people for superficial reasons, but after spending so many months living alone and reassessing what matters to me, true companionship is what I'm now seeking. A friend recently shared how the pause during lockdown forced her to really get to know the person she was dating. Prior to Covid, she tells me, she'd have been too busy to invest the time and would have likely not dated them long-term. But the slow pace of life, and with little else going on during lockdown, meant she had more time to get to know them. Her schedule wasn't getting in the way of this connection. A year later, she's in the happiest and healthiest relationship of her adult life. This made me reassess my own dating patterns and behaviours. Post-pandemic, I want to make the effort to really get to know someone rather than letting my work schedule get in the way. To switch off from the distractions of life, taking the time to be with someone and only them. Eliminating the myriad small interruptions. While this is easier said than done, I do want to try. It isn't about whether the person sweeps me off my feet or buys me flowers every week (although that would be nice); what matters is who they are in the world. How do they love those in their immediate circle, as well as those unknown to them by name?

Just thinking about dating through a pandemic is grim. Romance doesn't exactly come easily when you're not 100 per cent sure it's legal to meet up. And even then, you're not overly excited to kiss them because they could be asymptomatic with a virus that could potentially kill you both. It might seem a little *Romeo and Juliet*-esque but for most of us, it's not particularly appealing. Sure, you could have Zoom dates with a potential lover but how can you tell if the person on the small screen in front of you actually smells good? I'm serious. You can't know until you meet in person that they're not doused in Davidoff Cool Water circa 1999. Determining compatibility is about getting to know someone for more than just the vain stuff, yes. But non-verbal communication is just as important in the process of falling in love. Consider the opportunity to casually touch someone's forearm while they're talking. Or that lovely electric feeling when your thighs accidentally touch under the table. How are we meant to even know if we're attracted to someone if we can't play accidental footsies under the table at the pub? How do we evaluate them as a viable sexual partner without being able to check out their butt while they're leaning over a sticky bar to order us a round of house white? Getting to know someone is complicated as it is, let alone doing it from the waist up and staring into a camera on your phone. These things can sound light, silly and frivolous but they're not. They matter.

In the absence of being able to experience another human with all my senses, I opted for indefinite celibacy. Well, at least until the state's Chief Medical Officer, Brett Sutton, who himself became an unexpected sex symbol, gave us the all-clear. But for some of my girlfriends, an indefinite break from sex was unbearable, with some even threatening to violate lockdown restrictions. Heck, I didn't blame them. But how does anyone have sex safely during a global pandemic, when condoms are the least of your worries? In Victoria, Premier Dan Andrews found himself giving an awkward sex talk at one of his daily press briefings. The birds and bees wasn't great when our parents first delivered it but listening to Andrews explain why intimate partners didn't have to wear masks during lockdown took it to a whole new level. He said that 'the very nature of a platonic relationship between two people who are coming together to spend time with each other, that's very different to intimate partners, who by virtue of the fact that they are intimate partners, their contact is of a different nature.' The roomful of journalists tittered, while meme and TikTok makers everywhere cackled with glee. The health department of New South Wales created handy animated online resources[23] that encouraged people to find ways of being intimate while ensuring that no respiratory droplets were exchanged between partners. Our governments were advising us to have phone sex and masturbate as a way of keeping ourselves safe. These were strange and unusual times that absolutely nobody saw coming.

If getting sex advice from politicians was a low point, maybe there were some upsides in rethinking the way romantic or sexual partners get together. The pace of dating culture slowed down during the pandemic. Weekends couldn't be filled with back-to-back dates. Booty calls were basically cancelled. It all became rather Jane Austen-like, with new potential couples walking beside one another, hands clasped behind their backs and not touching. Chaperones, at least, weren't an option because walking as a group was often against the law. Prior to the pandemic, one of my male friends had a tendency to date lots of women at the same time, always looking for sex but rarely anything more meaningful or lasting. During lockdown, he was unusually taking the time to get to know one at a time, properly. He was initiating FaceTime dates and socially distanced catch-ups that allowed him and his date to actually get to know each other better. This, he later confided in me, was something that wouldn't have necessarily been possible before. There was an expectation, an attitude, and a set of assumptions that had developed around dating prior to the pandemic. People were there to be assessed, swiped, used and discarded. Sex was something that came first, rather than being built towards over time. The pandemic forced us to get back to the polite basics. Early reports suggested a surge in the number of downloads of dating apps with the onset of the pandemic.[24] Speaking to *Marie Claire Australia* in February 2021, Bumble's Asia-Pacific Communications Director, Lucille McCart, said, 'When lockdown restrictions were announced, it essentially flipped dating on its head and we quickly saw Bumble users shift to creating more meaningful connections online rather than in person.'[25]

These are all good signs, I reckon. Some of us single folks are hoping that it means dating culture will change for good. Maybe we will have the pandemic to thank for us ceasing to treat every prospective date as disposable and replaceable. Maybe we'll take more than a hot minute to get to know people, or be more open about what we want, or even just be gentler with other people's hearts. There are also dating practices and practicalities I'd quite like to see end up in the trash. Traditional twenty-first century dating can be expensive – a new lipstick, a wax, an Uber to the restaurant, dinner, drinks, a taxi to the next venue, maybe a movie or a sporting match, more drinks … it adds up. The pandemic has forced us to reassess who we want to spend our time with but also how we want to spend our money. Instead of feeling obliged to go on a date simply because it's a match, perhaps we'll start to re-evaluate. While face-to-face dates aren't going anywhere anytime soon, swiping right or left more thoughtfully might contribute to more meaningful connections. Perhaps we'll do away with the cold-hearted business of swiping altogether.

I didn't date during the lockdowns and now, when I go back to download the apps again, I pause. The memories of previous experiences turn me off completely. I do not miss men who say 'I've never dated a Black woman before' as though it was some kind of compliment, or having to listen to someone talk endlessly about themselves while mentally working out what the acceptable time limit was to make my exit. The pandemic made me see that the performance of dating deserves far less of my energy. I really don't have the time or the patience for that sort of thing.

Dating felt like hard work during lockdown, especially when it was hard enough to motivate myself to get through the basic tasks of keeping myself going during the day. I did worry that it might end up being a permanent state of being. That I'd have to adopt a lot of cats to keep me company, but the fear was fleeting. Besides, cats are great. If I am honest, I was mostly anxious about meeting up with new people because I might catch the virus. And as it turns out, I wasn't alone. A study in Canada[26] found that dating behaviours changed during Covid-19 because 'humans have evolved a set of subconscious responses that manifest when we are particularly concerned about the presence of an infectious disease.' The study continues, 'these responses lead us to engage in behavioural patterns that reduce the likelihood of getting infected, such as being less open and making reduced eye contact when in social situations.' In a dating context, the study found that people who felt more vulnerable to disease consistently displayed lower levels of interest in their prospective dates. I imagine that it will take us single people time to adjust and even feel comfortable with intimacy again. If epidemiologists are right and we live through more epidemics during our time on Earth, then maybe some of us will retreat and avoid dating altogether out of fear of getting sick. Maybe the logistics of early love have changed for good.

Angelica* says she cried like a Disney Princess when she first heard about lockdowns on the news. A self-described hopeless romantic, Angelica maintains that throwing herself on the bed and howling was not an overreaction. 'I've always been extra,' she says matter-of-factly. After thoroughly mourning the break-up of her previous five-year relationship, 2020 was going to be her year. Angelica said she finally felt ready to date again and was going at it with gusto. 'I was on every app there is, not for sex but to really meet someone. I believe in love even though I have been super unlucky again and again,' says Angelica. 'And again and again,' she adds for good measure. Determined not to lose a year in her search for love, Angelica began going on socially distanced walks with people in her Melbourne five-kilometre radius. 'I decided, because it could literally only lead to a walk, not even a kiss, to be more open-minded,' she explains. 'And not just saying it either, actually open-minded. I dated a tradie, a lawyer, a nurse and a consultant, whatever that is. I dated a woman who was ten years older than me and a guy who was five years younger. It felt safe, because why not? We were just talking.'

Some people did manage to find love in 2020 and Angelica was one of them. She met a woman who made her laugh and occasionally touched the small of her back in what felt like a delicious act of rule breaking. When the lockdown rules eased in Melbourne, they started to spend time together in one another's homes. Angelica met her new girlfriend's daughter and her cat and the rabbit, and said she was initially affronted by the mess and noise of a family home. 'It was a lot. Like, a *lot* a lot. I'd had months living and working on my own in a one-bedroom apartment with nothing to do except keep the place clean. Then I walked into Kelly's* place and it's this explosion of My Little Ponies and Hatchimals and dress-ups and leftovers and, like, half-constructed IKEA furniture. It was totally overwhelming at first but mostly because the contrast was so big. I was living a pretty small and quiet existence. But now I wouldn't change it,' says Angelica. 'In fact, I'm going to move into it,' she says with a kind of goofy grin.

Despite Angelica's happy experience, the logistics of extended lockdown weren't exactly conducive to romantic success. If you lived in different homes, there were long stretches of time where you couldn't see or touch each other, and you certainly weren't allowed to exchange bodily fluids. And if you did live together, you had to spend every waking second with that person. How did that affect our sex lives? A study from the University of Melbourne that surveyed 1000 people found that couples were having less sex during lockdown.[27] One of the factors, according to the report, was that the mental health toll of the pandemic had affected their desire to have sex. Another Australia-wide study found sexual activity declined during the lockdown restrictions across the country. Between new couples worrying about catching the virus and established couples exhausted by homeschooling and domestic labour, perhaps it's no surprise that so many of us weren't feeling sexy. Or perhaps in homes where you could barely find a moment to be alone, or in homes where you were only ever alone, we instead turned to pleasuring ourselves? The biggest song during the cursed year of 2020 was about vaginas. Cardi B and Megan Thee Stallion's smash-hit 'WAP' (an acronym for the less radio-friendly phrase 'Wet Ass Pussy') centres the vagina and encourages women to find the joy in fucking. Even celebrities got behind the empowering message and recorded TikToks of themselves dancing to the song. Everyone from Jennifer Lopez to Viola Davis[28] was into it. Other celebrities cashed in on the renewed focus on female pleasure, with Dakota Johnson, Lily Allen[29] and Abbie Chatfield[30] all spruiking their own signature vibrators.

During the first national lockdown, adult shops saw a surge in people buying sex toys.[31] A study by the Kinsey Institute at Indiana University found that sexual desire in relationships varied. Dr Justin Lehmiller, a research fellow at the Institute, told CNN: 'Some people reported their sex lives and romantic lives had improved and were reporting their relationships were better and stronger than ever,' he said. 'But a larger number reported challenges in their sex lives and relationships.'[32] Interestingly, while some people were having less sex, others were getting more adventurous with their sexual activities. The Kinsey report tells us that people living with their partners were more likely to try new sexual positions and act on their sexual fantasies. Despite the challenges thrown their way by the pandemic, some people found creative ways to satisfy their sexual desires and needs. Perhaps it had to take a global pandemic for people to feel less embarrassed about it. For too long, women have been socialised to be ashamed about our bodies, and our sexuality has often taken a backseat despite our foremothers advocating for our sexual liberation during the sexual revolution of feminism's second wave in the sixties and seventies. Maybe 'WAP' wasn't exactly what they envisaged when they lobbied for the legalisation of abortion, but it was always about 'women's health and women's sexuality together'.[33] They fought for their right to be safe, healthy and sexually satisfied.

Look, I never expected one of the nicest outcomes of a global pandemic to be that we were more open to female sexuality, but I'll take it.

Huynh* and her husband approached lockdown with the order and planning they brought to everything. 'We had a spreadsheet,' admits Huynh. 'It's such a cliché,' she says with her head between her hands. Huynh and her husband are both Sydney-based actuaries, and with two children under six suddenly at home full-time, a timetable of who and when everyone was working and caring for children sounded kind of sensible.

But even Excel-level planning wasn't enough to keep the arguments out of their household. Huynh describes a steady descent into bickering that started to stray into resentment. 'We're Asian. We don't talk about feelings,' she says. 'But we needed to. My husband has a respiratory condition, so we kept our children at home to be safe. We wore masks even when we didn't have to while outside and inside, our home was very tense.' Huynh appears uncomfortable while describing the more intimate parts of her family life. 'I don't know if we were normal or not, but we would fight most weeks,' she says. 'I would try not to say anything until the children were asleep but sometimes our shouting woke them up. We have never fought much in the past. I think in the pandemic, it became too much. We stopped repressing and started arguing instead and I don't think it was good for us. I felt so sad most of 2020. It is easier now the children are back at school and day care, and we go into the office to work but the wound is open now, you know? I don't know how we will fix it, the resentment.'

As Huynh's story proves, it wasn't just sex and how to reimagine intimacy that challenged relationships during the pandemic. People spent more time with their partners than they ever had before, and this came with both advantages and disadvantages. For some, it was too much. Hours on end spent together exposed cracks in the relationship, leading to break-ups. In Sweden, the number of divorce filings increased during the pandemic.[34] In Australia, the number of marriages fell by more than 30 per cent in the first six months of 2020,[35] in part because of restrictions causing people to delay their nuptials. A study by Relationships Australia[36] found that close to 60 per cent of people were challenged by their living arrangements during lockdown. It also found that 42 per cent of people had experienced a negative change in their relationship with their partner in that period. Being cooped up with a significant other for days and months on end was not easy and the patience of many couples was tested. But not every disagreement turned into a relationship breakdown.

According to world-renowned psychotherapist Esther Perel, fighting is a normal part of any relationship. In an interview with *The New Yorker*, she argued that *how* people fight is what matters: 'When you get really mad at something, can you afterward say, "O.K., got that out of my system – how are we going to solve this?" or "Look, I realise I was quite unfair. Let me first say what I *do* appreciate about what you do before I dump on you the whole list of stuff that I don't think you do?"'[37] That advice will be relevant long after the pandemic has left us. It's even possible that some couples will have learned better conflict resolutions skills during this weird time, which is probably a lesser-known upside of having a global pandemic. For others, the lack of solutions, or the lack of shared commitment to finding a solution, will irrevocably damage relationships. Some social psychologists predict a spike in relationship breakdowns over the next few years as couples face up to the reality of their pandemic-induced frustrations with one another. Others say that the coming years will likely be a time of healing and adjustment that most couples will make it through.

I know what you've been thinking as you read the paragraphs above: what about the cheaters? Won't anyone think of the cheaters? People trying to conduct extramarital affairs under some of the strictest lockdown restrictions in the world really had their work cut out for them. There have been reports suggesting there was a decline in workplace affairs,[38] which makes sense when the office was barred for so many people. Perel argues that this dire lack of cheating opportunities may have forced some couples to reconnect with the person they're legally bound to. 'For people who do have another partner and can't go see that person right now, I think what's happening is that, in some cases, people are reconnecting with their partner and disconnecting from their external interests, and, in other cases, people are disconnecting from their partners and becoming more eager to connect with all the other opportunities that they may have on the outside.'

Like many things in life, friendships weren't untouched by the pandemic. For some, conspiracy theory rants on social media were enough to sever ties. If you lived in Melbourne during lockdown, perhaps some friends in other parts of the country living mask-free lives and throwing parties forced us to hit the unfollow button on Instagram. The reasons for friendships not being able to survive the pandemic are complicated and varied. Being forced to reassess our lives, many of us realised that we tolerated behaviour pre-Covid that we weren't keen to put up with during a global pandemic. With the crisis taking its toll, we found ourselves clashing with friends whose values and attitudes no longer aligned with our own. As hard as it is to see a friendship come to an end, these audits are important for our own growth. Being able to place boundaries on what is and isn't acceptable behaviour is important, or so my therapist tells me. Following the global Black Lives Matter protests, I started reassessing many close interracial friendships. I'm no longer interested in being friends with anyone who either refuses to engage with conversations around race or is dismissive of these experiences. This isn't a hard and fast rule: I'm aware some friends are still learning and may not know what to say, and that's okay. But in the companionships where I felt I was constantly having to justify my humanity, I realised that no amount of patience, explaining, or avoidance was going to save these friendships. It hasn't been easy and, in the process, I've had to let go of some people from life.

The time inside taught me a valuable lesson in who and what I wanted to invest my time in. I wanted to go, and be, where I was loved. And to be loved is to be seen and to be accepted for who you are. And it seems, I'm not alone. The lockdowns put strains on friendships, with a French survey[39] finding that while some relationships improved, others just weren't able to sustain the impact of lockdowns. The preliminary results of the research found that many people turned to their close friends and family for support, contributing to other friendships fizzling out. This 'funnelling effect' saw many of us prioritising the relationships we valued most. In my case, some of the friendships that didn't withstand the pressures of a global pandemic and a civil rights movement were people who I thought I had strong bonds with. And to my surprise, I grew closer to people who, prior to Covid, I'd seen only as acquaintances. And while some of these changes to our social networks may be temporary, as research suggests,[40] the reminder for me was that even in the most unexpected of circumstances, we're able to form new bonds. That's worth holding on to well after the pandemic is over.

Despite the meaning I've tried to find from many lockdowns, I know not everyone felt so emotionally connected. 'People are spending *a lot* more time on porn right now,' said Esther Perel in the midst of the pandemic. She's correct. There was a significant increase in the number of people accessing pornography and also adult chat websites.[41] Now, according to Perel,[42] infidelity means different things to different people, so maybe these activities were an infraction in some households and of no remark in others. 'The whole issue with modern infidelity [is that] you can have a full-blown affair with somebody while you're lying next to your partner in bed. So, there's not that much of a change in that respect,' she explains. It's easy to draw a picture of the emotional impact of the pandemic in simplistic bold lines. But that doesn't make it an accurate depiction. Human beings and their relationships are deeply complex. The inability to be physically proximate to your lover doesn't mean that connection cannot flourish in other ways. Just as engaging with pornography for a private sexual release doesn't mean the absence of love for the person you get to sleep beside each night. Conversations of love and sex weren't priorities for many couples prior to the pandemic. Perhaps in its wake, having been forced to spend considerable time alone together, couples will find new urgency to have conversations of importance.

Fortunately, living on my own, there was zero chance of my springing a partner watching porn in the study. My personal emptiness stemmed from a different source. I started to notice how much I craved being physically touched by another human being. Not in a sexual way, even; but just being held and being hugged tightly so I could feel the warmth from the other person. At some point, I was listening to a BBC radio program[43] on which a psychologist suggested people could teach themselves to 'self-hug'. Professor Merle Fairhurst from the Bundeswehr University in Munich told people to 'imagine the last hug they had and then to wrap their arms around themselves in a self-hug which they then hold for two minutes.' I reluctantly tried it. My verdict is that it was embarrassing, even on my own. Maybe mildly comforting for a moment, but nowhere near as good as nuzzling into another person. Not knowing when I'd be able to experience touch again was what made me feel truly alone during the pandemic. This sensation is called touch starvation, that intense craving we have for touch. According to researchers at the Texas Medical Center,[44] 'when someone is touch starved, it's like someone who is starved for food. They want to eat, but they can't. Their psyche and their body want to touch someone, but they can't do it because of the fear associated with, in this case, the pandemic.' This starvation, the researchers argue, can lead to psychological issues including depression and anxiety.

South African writer and filmmaker Milisuthando Bongela is a friend of mine. She once told me that humans weren't designed to be alone. As a descendant of the Xhosa people in present-day South Africa, Milli told me about a philosophy called ukukhapha. It's this idea that, culturally, someone is always beside you, and you are never truly alone. When you move through the world, whether you like it or not, an ancestor or relative will always accompany you through every stage of life. Whether going on a trip, visiting someone's home, or getting up on stage to deliver a speech, someone always accompanies you, she told me. The point of the practice is to not *be* alone, even if we *feel* alone. Milli explained this all to me late one night in her Johannesburg apartment. During 2020, I caught myself wondering if we could possibly have ukukhapha during lockdown. What does it mean to show up for people during a pandemic?

How much is enough? How can we be there for someone emotionally even when we cannot be there physically?

As the crisis dragged on, groups and organisations were created to respond to the impact isolation was having on people. One such initiative in Australia was the #ViralKindness movement, which describes itself as a network of community care groups across Australia that support neighbours in need or isolation during the Covid-19. Set up by the political advocacy group GetUp!, it was inspired by a postcard initiative in Britain, which offered practical support for people self-isolating. 'There were quite a few community groups who were already jumping in and trying to organise this level of care in their neighbourhood. And then there were other people who wanted to help but didn't have any existing structure or connections,' Susie Gemmell from GetUp! tells me. Gemmell says that these groups were all 'centralised' on their website. The premise was quite simple: an organisation would list itself on the #ViralKindness website and download a postcard template. These postcards would then be placed in their neighbours' letterboxes to help with everyday tasks from collecting groceries and medication to dog walking. Gemmell says it was a way for people to show up for those most at risk. 'Some people approached it from a very practical standpoint of wanting to make sure that anyone in their community, particularly elderly people who were frightened of contracting the virus or who just couldn't get out and had lost their regular support networks, [was supported],' she said.

Inspired by this, I decided to start my own kindness movement. I started sending postcards to strangers who would send direct messages to me on Instagram, posting care packages to family, and calling friends I hadn't spoken to in a very long time. It shifted my experience of lockdown. Kindness feels nice. One of the people on my list of friends who I hadn't spoken to in years was Milli. We'd exchanged the occasional text every now and again, but we just hadn't found the time to properly check in on each other. Such is the gift of love that regardless of how much time has lapsed, we both felt so at ease we could pick up where we'd left off with each other. We spoke via Skype – her in South Africa, me in Australia. I'd hoped we'd discuss ukukhapha, this philosophy of what it means to show up for each other, but the conversation became a meditation on grief and dying. 'Every single day, we get a message that someone we know has died from Covid,' Milli says. 'And so the question of your own mortality then gets put right in front of you.' Milli had contracted Covid-19 and the practicality of dealing with potentially dying became her focus. 'I had to write my banking details, this is where all my insurance policies are, this is who to call if you have to report my death,' she told me. When her sisters and mother also contracted Covid, Milli gave them the same advice.

While Milli and her sisters were spared the worst of Covid, their mother ended up in intensive care. 'I remember packing a suitcase of my clothes and I asked myself, "Do I have to pack a black dress?" and I stood in front of my wardrobe considering this. "Is she going to die? Other people's mums have died, why wouldn't she?" And the ability to live through that fear was only possible because we were there for each other,' Milli says. She tells me that despite being the most scared she's even been in her life, she also felt a lot of love. 'We also experienced as much – if not more – love from each other, from her, from other family members, from the community, from people that know her. It stretches you completely, you open.' Thankfully, her mum survived and as I sit and listen from the other side of the world, I realise that in that moment, we're both showing up for each other. Milli and I are beside one another, through this hardship, present despite our physical distance. Perhaps this was ukukhapha for modern times.

Thinking about death, dying and grief, I searched for information about how to cope. Death is a taboo subject, and despite it being a likely outcome of a fatal pandemic, we still weren't talking enough about it. Australia's death tolls were mercifully low compared to other countries around the world, but watching the news really brought home how terrifying the situation was beyond our closed borders. At the beginning, Australians were told about the people who contracted the virus as well as the offenders who were spreading it. Names and even faces graced our television screens, giving us a human being to connect with and care about. These profiles humanised the experience of Covid-19, reminding us that the people who got sick or died were also someone's mother, daughter, son, neighbour, colleague or friend. That they were loved. But as the death toll mounted, these stories of the lives that these people lived and the loved ones they left behind became more infrequent. Perhaps we were too scared to ask what others' experiences were. Perhaps it was easier to be angry at the situation than confront the emotionally complex reality. Perhaps there were simply too many stories of death to be told; too many stories of death to take in. Regardless of the reason, we came to understand the tragedy en masse rather than at the individual level. We counted cases and deaths at the daily press conferences, graphed the scale of disaster in neat diagrams on the nightly news, and lost part of ourselves and our innocent souls in the process.

In a pandemic journal for the *New York Times*, American writer Teju Cole put it simply: 'People are dying in hospitals and dying at home. The official tolls are almost certainly an undercount. The morgues are overflowing. Those are the facts. But where is the grief?'[45] Where – literally – could we put our grief? The restrictions imposed by the pandemic meant that people couldn't grieve safely together. Rituals that help us cope with the pain of losing loved ones like funerals and wakes were almost impossible to organise or attend. Instead, people had to find new ways of saying goodbye, complicating and stagnating the grieving process. While grief looks different for everyone, it looks terribly odd during a pandemic. One friend described to me sitting on her bed, watching a funeral on Zoom. She had dressed for the occasion, swapping her usual lockdown tracksuit for some jeans and a shirt. In the middle of the service, her son came into the room with a toy that needed fixing. She went to tell him to leave before realising that there was nothing stopping her from multitasking in her grief.

Monica Smith knows the acute pain of not being able to see or touch someone she loved during their final moments. Monica is based in the United States but has children living across the world. When the pandemic started, she tells me via video call from New Jersey, Monica was still in Australia visiting family. 'I came home at the end of 2019 because my mother had been in care since 2010 and my stepfather was in his late 90s. [Before the pandemic] I would come home a couple of times a year to spend time with them,' Monica says. The 2019–2020 trip was a much sadder one than usual. Her stepfather died at the start of the new year, a few months before the pandemic took hold. Monica's husband had already returned home, and she decided to stay in Australia for a few more months in the hope that things would get better. She moved in with her son and daughter-in-law for company but once it became clear that things weren't going to improve for a while, she opted to return to the United States. Before she left, Monica went to visit her mother, who was living in an aged care facility in Geelong. 'I did get to see Mum before I left. My brother and I went in and they had screens up and we got tested and Mum was behind the glass screen. She had no idea what was going on.' That was the last time Monica saw her mother. Back in America, a few months later, she was called by the nursing home to be present online as her mother passed. In ordinary circumstances, Monica would have flown back to Australia for the funeral. That wasn't an option.

Monica hopes to retire in Australia one day with her husband but with children and grandchildren flung to the far corners of the world, settling anywhere for long seems complex and lonely. When Monica's mother died, it was a goodbye made on a screen. So was her video conference funeral. To me, it's unspeakably harrowing. I can only imagine how odd and how deep the grief must have been, saying goodbye to someone so many kilometres away and then simply having to get on with the business of living through a pandemic. What space is there for grief like that and how do we possibly live with it? But Monica is stoic. She says that she was still 'in the room when she died' because of technology. 'It was as good as it could possibly be and it was always a natural progression,' she tells me. This seems an awfully brave and generous way for someone to describe the experience of watching their mother die over Zoom. What other choice does she have but to deal with this brutal reality though? How we all contend with these things will affect the way we cope and live and love each other as we move on from the pandemic. Let us hope Zoom is contained only to meetings, not moments of love and grief, in future.

Maria Stamelos has been privy to grief like Monica's rather a lot this past year. Perhaps even more than usual, as manager of a funeral business. Maria owns Victoria Funerals with her husband and she tells me she ends up acting as a pseudo-therapist for loved ones of the dead. The meetings where she asks the bereaved to provide information about the person who they've just lost feels like an ad hoc counselling session. 'It's therapeutic,' says Maria. 'A lot of the time, they go into the history of the person, and we get a lot of background that seems to be very helpful for them to talk about.' Maria's business deals with various cultural and religious requirements and a lot of their clients are Greek Orthodox. Greek Orthodox funerals are characterised by tradition. 'A viewing can take place in either our chapel or the church. But the service itself can only take place in the church,' Maria says. Pandemic restrictions made upholding these rituals challenging. 'The most difficult part, to be honest, is the fact that those who did pass away from Covid, we were not allowed to dress them or to have a viewing at all,' Maria explains. For Greek Orthodox families, being able to see their loved one in an open casket and spend time with them is a significant part of the grieving process. These processes, Maria tells me, are vital in helping people deal with their grief. 'It's not for the deceased, it's for all those left behind who have to deal with their grief and work through it,' she says. 'Even relatives and friends dropping in on the family of the deceased to pay their respects. Even that was disrupted. All of the support that people usually have, most of it disappeared.'

Grief craves ritual. It craves company and community and comfort and touch and tiny sandwiches on a table at the wake, and a fridge full of casseroles for the weeks ahead. What Maria described to me felt like disrupted grief, and even in her brave-faced positivity, what Monica described did too. It's a sort of suspended grief, cut off from the coping mechanisms we've developed over so many years. Covid has changed the logistics of our sadness and that must have been devastating and lonely for millions of people around the world. We may have come up with new ways to memorialise the dead, but they are a patch on what we had before. As I write this, Indian citizens are burning bodies on mass funeral pyres because the crematoriums are full. One particular heartbreaking image brought me to tears – it showed a mother sitting with the lifeless body of her son at her feet in a rickshaw as she travelled from hospital to hospital, hoping to have him admitted, and turned away because they were at capacity. He died on his way to a third hospital. The impact of seeing your loved one's body dealt with as part of a conveyor belt of corpses is indefinable. Psychologists and sociologists make their predictions as to how this altered grief will shape us as individuals in the long-term. They cannot say how exactly, but they are sure that it will.

I worry about where this cumulative and collective grief will end up. How will it affect our abilities to work, and to maintain healthy relationships and our health and overall wellbeing?

Dr Harvey Chochinov is a professor of psychiatry at Manitoba University in Canada, and in an interview with PRI, he said, 'We can really expect that there is going to be a tsunami of suffering,' as a result of this grief. According to Dr Chochinov, this prolonged bereavement could lead to an increase in people suffering from persistent complex bereavement disorder,[46] which is accompanied by anxiety, PTSD, sleep disorders and depression. In May 2020, experts in grief and bereavement lobbied the Canadian government to create a national grief strategy to tackle the pandemic-related grief.

Before the pandemic, I would have described myself as someone who loved solitude. While that remains true to some degree, I did notice that during lockdowns, I wasn't just physically alone, I was also lonely. I was initially somewhat ashamed to admit this, as an independent woman who likes to think she can do things for herself. In my confusion, I turned to an expert, Dr Michelle Lim, to understand why I had lost some of my love for being alone. Dr Lim studies loneliness at Swinburne University and says there is indeed a distinction between feeling lonely and being alone. The two are 'related', but they also occur independently. 'Loneliness by definition is subjective,' says Dr Lim. 'It is very much a feeling, so you can be among people – you can be working, you can be living in a family, you can be married – but still feel like people don't understand you.' Dr Lim found that as the level of social restrictions increased, many people reported that they felt lonelier. 'In one study that we did looking at the start of Australia's first wave of Covid outbreak, we asked people if they felt lonelier after the restrictions were implemented. One in two people mentioned that they felt more lonely,' she says. Furthermore, marginalised people tend to be more vulnerable to loneliness. 'People of a lower socio-economic background, people who have caring responsibilities, people who live in more deprived neighbourhoods are really the ones that suffer,' says Dr Lim. Estimates indicate that about 10 per cent of the population are described as chronically lonely.

Pandemic loneliness hit women more than men, according to one study in the United States.[47] In many cultural communities here in Australia, being surrounded by extended families and networks is important for women's wellbeing in particular. These social bonds are central to many migrant and refugee women and according to research by the University of Melbourne, Covid-19 disproportionately affected disadvantaged communities[48] such as these. Diana Sayed, chief executive of the Australian Muslim Women's Centre for Human Rights, says, 'Our biggest fear was isolation for women in terms of the programs we run in communities because we're in schools with young women, we're running programs with Syrian, Afghan, and other migrant and refugee women.' She tells me that these programs are a 'big form of connection' for women to meet other women with shared experience. For many Muslim women, 'collectivism' is at the heart of the familial experience. 'It's not the fact that we live with our immediate family, we also have in-laws, we also have our own parents, brothers, sisters; we live in sort of larger communal households,' Sayed explains. How can you restrict people to only interacting with the household unit when the family unit is actually so much bigger? What impact does that have on each person's mental health and coping capacity? And for those who live with one large family group to a single dwelling, what does this mean for their safety? Culturally appropriate support is vital for women from these communities and ensuring that the organisations that support them are adequately resourced post-pandemic is essential. It's evident that these women rely on these networks and communities and being unable to access this care impacts their wellbeing.

As if it wasn't enough dealing with isolation, grief and loneliness, Australian women were also expected to be having more babies for the sake of our economy. In July 2020, just months into this whole ordeal, Federal Treasurer Josh Frydenberg instructed Australian women to get on with the business of having more babies. Breeding to grow the economic pie. In his post-budget speech, Frydenberg said that 'people should feel encouraged about the future and the more children that we have across the country, together with our migration, we will build our population growth and that will be good for the economy.'[49] Now, economic stimulation is not exactly the most compelling reason to procreate, but the treasurer gave it a try. For young couples all over the country, it felt jarring and simplistic. In the midst of a global pandemic that was still raging across the world – and was yet to reach its peak – babies were the furthest thing from so many people's minds. Not to mention the concerns regularly raised by young people, unsure about starting a family because of the costs of raising a child and the enormous uncertainty surrounding that child's future as a result of dangerous climate change. Personally, I found the treasurer's efforts rather amusing. I wasn't remotely convinced that this was the right time for me to be bringing new humans into the world.

Frydenberg's rallying cry brought back memories of another treasurer, alarmed by the declining fertility rate, urging Australians to 'have one for mum, one for dad and one for the country'. Almost two decades earlier, Peter Costello offered financial incentives to entice Australians to reproduce and, for a short moment in time, it had an impact. But things have changed considerably since. The state of the world, for one, as well as our capacity to hope and plan for the future.

Historically, women without children have been persecuted, shunned, or even divorced. Feminist icon Gloria Steinem, herself childfree, has described this stigma as sexist.[50] In an interview, Steinem was asked whether she thought she'd been judged for not having children. 'I think so, in a way that people assume that I must be unhappy or unfulfilled,' she said. 'Not everyone, but some people I think assume that – in a way that they wouldn't assume about a man.'

I struggle to ethically justify having children. It didn't help that in the same month that Frydenberg was drumming up support for more babies, the global Black Lives Matter movement was dominating Australia's news consumption. The movement brought into sharp focus the ongoing impact of systemic racism on communities of colour in the United States especially but also around the world. I navigate the world in a Black body and racism continues to impact my life. I have fears about my own children being exposed to the racism that I and members of my family know too well. I still recall the conversations my parents had with my brother and I as children. They tried to explain that some 'bad people' will say 'bad and mean things' to us and to be ready. The thought of having that same conversation decades later with my own children is awful. And living with the constant fear that my children could be killed simply because of the colour of their skin is enough to make me question having those children in the first place.

One of my girlfriends, Jess, fell pregnant for the first time unexpectedly during the pandemic. When I spoke to her, she was preparing for maternity leave as her due date was fast approaching. Jess is a Sydney-based audio producer, and she tells me that the forced isolation gave her time to adjust to her new normal. 'There was really this moment where I had to adjust to the idea and I felt like I could do that with a lot of privacy and time and space,' Jess says. I ask her if she is anxious about bringing a human into the world at this moment. 'It's a really difficult one to answer while pregnant,' Jess explains. 'It's really hard to think about these big ideas while you're pregnant. I definitely had a lot of anxiety about it before I was pregnant, and it took up a huge amount of my brain space.'

Giving birth is a scary experience for many women. During the pandemic, birth became not only terrifying but traumatic. There were hundreds of Australian women who were not allowed to have their partners with them for some or all of their birthing experience. Imagine being left alone, separated from the person who you will raise your child with, to bring that baby into the world?

Having a child during a pandemic meant that a lot of brand-new babies weren't able to meet their grandparents, aunts, uncles, cousins and assorted other doting adults. We've all seen photographs in news stories from around the world of elderly couples having to wave desperately at their fresh grandkids through a window, unable to cradle them or sniff the top of their little heads for fear of exchanging germs. If babies arrived during lockdowns, it meant the parents were more alone in that tender newborn phase than ever before. While this might have been sweet for some, it would also have been completely terrifying for others.

I am somewhat ambivalent and unsure about having children. How am I supposed to make this, one of the most important decisions of my life, when I don't even know what the first days of a baby's life could look like? I don't know. And I may continue not to know until that decision is made for me.

Some women forged ahead with plans to expand their families, both alone and with a partner, in spite of the gloomy economic projections. But then lockdown measures put a pause on elective surgeries, including fertility treatments, leaving many plans in limbo. Dr Fleur Cattrall, a fertility specialist at Melbourne IVF, says some treatments had to be stopped mid-cycle. 'Having to tell someone that they can't proceed with their treatment when they are close to forty or close to the end of their reproductive years … not knowing when they were going to be able to return to treatment was very difficult for us.' Once restrictions eased, fertility clinics saw a surge in the number of people seeking treatment to help them conceive. 'We became incredibly busy, and it was not what we were expecting at all. We thought that we would be very quiet,' she says. Dr Cattrall believes those who had been delaying seeking assistance thought it was a good time because of flexibility with work. The changed conditions for many office workers meant some women felt more confident they could balance employment and family, which is a really positive outcome. The lockdowns were also a contributor to the rise in egg freezing requests because single women 'weren't able to socialise', as Dr Cattrall puts it.

I asked Dr Cattrall if there is ever a right age for women to start exploring their fertility options. It's a controversial and prickly subject for some. She replied that 'if they're waiting for the right relationship and that's not happening by the age of about thirty-three, then it would be a good time to at least consult with a fertility specialist to get some more information.' I wonder whether women should adjust their timelines because of Covid-19? Many of us have lost critical decision-making years, myself included. With epidemiologists predicting that pandemics could become more common in the future, how can we be confident about accessing fertility treatments if and when we want to? The truth is that we cannot. And when your ticking biological clock is suddenly going off and you're consumed by emotions and second-guessing all of your life choices? It's not the best time to be told that you can no longer access the health care you require to conceive. I'm angry about the burden of responsibility women carry and the pain that often comes with doing so. Every decision women make comes with its own set of challenges. And now we have added a new one: trying to find the mental capacity and courage and clarity to move forward – or not – in the midst of a global pandemic.

Australian women are having fewer babies than ever before. In 2019, our national fertility rate dropped to its lowest level in more than a century to 1.66 live births per woman. That is well below the so-called replacement rate of 2.1 live births per woman, which hasn't been seen in our country since the 1970s. At the start of Covid-19, experts predicted that Australia would see a fertility boom, with articles and memes about so-called 'lockdown babies' giving us the impression that everyone was getting ready to reproduce. While the impact of the pandemic on the birthrate is not yet being reported, there is little real evidence to suggest this could be true. Demographer Dr Liz Allen says there was a misconception that because people were spending more time at home, it'd result in more pregnancies. 'A baby boom is not just about time or even more babies. It's about the rates of fertility,' Dr Allen explains. Quite simply, for a baby boom to occur, there must be more partnering and less use of contraceptive devices. During the last baby boom in Australia, there were young men returning from World War II, young women desperate to start families, money was plentiful during the reconstruction boom, and we hadn't invented contraception yet. But in 2020? 'We didn't run out of condoms,' states Dr Allen simply. 'We didn't see sales of the oral contraceptive pill decline. We didn't have an issue of supply.'

Women get the blame for declining fertility rates. Rather than recognising that reproduction is a choice made by couples more often than it is by individuals, we point fingers at women. Underlying these accusatory tones that dominate public conversation and consciousness is the outdated idea that women's only role is to breed and raise children. 'Whenever we talk about fertility rates, we're talking about women,' says Dr Allen. 'We're not talking about men and women. It all comes down to how many births per woman embedded in the calculations.' I suggest that regardless of what choice women make, they are damned if they do or damned if they don't and Dr Allen agrees. 'If women aren't having enough babies, they're called selfish,' she says. 'The "wrong" kind of woman is having too many babies and the "right" kind of woman is having too few. We always focus on women.'

If Australia is genuinely worried about falling fertility rates – and we should be – then we need to be focused on the factors that caused them in the first place. Things like poverty, economic inequality, financial security, unemployment, the ease with which women can transition in and out of the workforce, the accessibility and affordability of childcare, and the gender pay gap, to name a few. Parenthood might seem like an extremely personal decision but it's a political issue. Birthing babies was complicated before the pandemic and now, it is even more complicated.

'If we look at survey data, it suggests that couples are actually not achieving their desired family size. Why? Because life gets in the way,' says Dr Allen. Usually that's things like a career, ageing parents, financial concerns, moral deliberations, too many good dates, indecision, fertility problems. Add to this the limitations on intimacy, access to medical care and confusion of living through a pandemic. Dr Allen says the burden hits women the hardest. 'Something's gotta give and so we adjust our fertility intentions down.'

Dr Allen's insights don't come as a surprise to me. They're pretty much backed up by the conversations I've been having with my friends. Many of my girlfriends are aged in their thirties and yet to have children, with reasons ranging from climate change to the high cost of living and parenting. We're still trying to work out how we'll be able to afford our own homes let alone bringing new people into them. Dr Allen says, 'we're now faced with the prospect that, at an individual level, people might be childless not because they want to be without children, but because life is too difficult to have children and to also have everything else.' In an economy that urgently needs the birthrate to climb, this feels like an utterly hopeless and underdone area of public policy.

The pandemic has potentially devastating implications on Australian mothers' capacity to cope. Chloé Brugalé was one of millions of women navigating parenting duties during the pandemic. She has two children under the age of eighteen and shared the caring and domestic duties with her partner. 'The biggest challenge came around carrying a lot of hats,' Brugalé tells me. 'I was not just the mum. I had to be the teacher. I had to be their friend because they weren't in contact with other children, and I had to become the mental health carer. I had to be the entertainer. I had to be the sports coach. I became this person who had to wear so many hats for them, as well the ones I wear in my own life.' Brugalé's children had individual and very different needs. One is a teenager and the other a toddler. She tells me that initially, navigating life in lockdown wasn't so bad. 'The first lockdown, where we were not restricted by distance, was actually quite good because as a family, we made the most of it. We would go somewhere we'd never been every weekend.' But as lockdown wore on, and restrictions got harsher in Melbourne, the family's enthusiasm to take on new challenges evaporated. 'We felt like we were in a fishbowl,' Brugalé says. 'We were looking at how other people were coping and there were all these creative projects with children, you could see people baking, people starting gardens and I was inspired,' she says. But ultimately, it got overwhelming keeping up with all the demands on her time. 'I'd be walking in the street and someone had created a gratitude tree where people were posting what they were grateful for and someone else created a fairy garden. At the start of the lockdowns I thought, "look at this, this is great", and at the end I was just like, "fuck them". I just can't do it.' Then guilt started to creep in. And in this, she wasn't alone.

Parenting guilt got worse during lockdown. One study conducted by British label manufacturer My Nametags[51] found that women were more likely to experience increased guilt, with mums afflicted by guilt eight times more per month than dads. The most common reasons for feeling guilty during lockdown was just how bored their children were, followed by their inability to spend time with relatives and keeping the children indoors all the time. Nina is a mother of one who lives with her partner in the south-eastern suburbs of Melbourne. She says the strain on her relationship with her partner as they tried to juggle the competing demands of lockdown were exhausting. They would take care of their daughter in shifts, swapping for her PR meetings on Zoom and his IT development chats on Microsoft Teams. They got by but Nina says she was more upset by the impact on her child and haunted by the sense she wasn't doing enough for her. 'James, my partner, just got on with it and wasn't bothered by our daughter watching hours and hours of ABC Kids. He'd just plonk her down whenever he needed to, and not really give it another thought.' Nina was doing painting and making treasure hunts and baking cupcakes with her daughter whenever she could but then she'd fall behind at work and find herself up late in the evenings trying to catch up. Her exhaustion gave way to a constant feeling of light-headedness and fuelled a newfound parenting anxiety.

'I became one of those "Instagram mums" almost by accident,' says Nina. 'We were doing so many activities and projects that when Nina looked cute or did something well, I wanted to post about it. I was proud of her, and I don't think there is anything really wrong with that.' But as time went on Nina caught herself looking at friends' social media and feeling competitive that maybe she wasn't 'doing enough'. She looks at her fingernails and scrunches up her mouth.

'I am not even sure competitive is the right word. I wasn't competing, I was trying to keep up. But the more I looked, the more I felt that I was letting my child down and not giving her the lockdown care and attention she deserved. Simultaneously, though, I was contributing to the whole fucking sordid mess of it by posting what we were doing. I mean, it's not like I was putting up photos of all those times she watched *Ben and Holly's Little Kingdom* on the iPad.'

Nina's partner, James, simply did not succumb to the same pressure to be a 'perfect parent', because for him it didn't exist. The pandemic magnified the patriarchal expectations we apply to mums that dads do not experience in the same way. Whether we like it or not, Australian's notion of womanhood is defined by motherhood, whereas masculinity is more closely associated with power and money.

The many gains of feminism were threatened during the pandemic because women picked up the bulk of additional unpaid labour. According to a report by the United Nations, women saw a larger increase in unpaid work compared to men and the pandemic reinforced traditional and social gender norms. The report, which analysed data from thirty-eight countries, found that in Australia, women were undertaking 1.8 times more unpaid work than before the pandemic.[52] Between juggling homeschooling, childcare and cleaning the house more regularly (because when nobody leaves them, houses get filthy really fast), Australian women become trapped in a never-ending cycle of additional responsibility. In an interview with the BBC, UN Women Deputy Executive Director Anita Bhatia warned of the ripple effects this has. 'It matters because if they're [women] doing more work, it means they're not doing something else,' she said. 'And if they're not doing something else, that typically means they're not earning an income and if they're not standing on their own two feet, they don't have financial independence and they are not contributing to their family's income, to the community and to the country.'[53] During the pandemic, women globally were spending on average three times as many hours on unpaid domestic and caring work than men, or 76 per cent of the total amount of unpaid labour.[54] While this varies geographically, here in Australia women were spending about 64 per cent of their average working hours each week on unpaid work, compared to just 36 per cent for men.[55]

In a survey of parents across the United States, Britain, France, Germany and Italy, 60 per cent said that they had no outside help in caring for and educating their children. A further 10 per cent said that they had some help, but it was less than before the pandemic. The report conducted by the Boston Consulting Group also found that parents were spending an additional twenty-seven hours each week on household chores, childcare and education.[56] Our modern economies are built not only on the unpaid labour of women but the paid labour of women. The vast majority of schoolteachers, early childhood educators and nannies are women. These were the individuals charged with supporting parents to raise the next generation, a vitally important and skilled contribution. And yet, despite their critical importance, these professions are generally underpaid. This is historical and flows from old-fashioned notions about women being drawn to caring work for love rather than money.

While men did take up more housework during lockdowns, women did even more. A survey conducted by the Australian Bureau of Statistics[57] shows that nearly 45 per cent of all women with children spent more than five hours each week supervising or caring for them and that more than a third spent more than twenty hours. Compare this with just 32 per cent of men spending more than five hours a week caring for children, and a mere 17 per cent spending more than twenty hours a week watching over or caring for their children. For all the optimistic talk of men spending more time with children and realising the burden their female partners carried, there has been little impact. Men did less unpaid child-caring before the pandemic, they did less during the pandemic, and they do less now. Despite men having a greater insight into just how much of the load women were carrying, it wasn't enough to get most of them to step up around the home. It seems that not even a deadly health crisis can change these deeply ingrained cultural attitudes.

The pandemic also underlined the vital role extended families play in supporting parents – from grandparents to aunties and uncles to friends – and how mothers rely on these networks to help spread the burden of unpaid labour. In the absence of these support structures, women took on more, despite the fact that for those who were coupled, the men were there and still not carrying their fair share of the domestic labour. If a pandemic couldn't get men to step up in an equitable way, what will? The pandemic made the pre-existing injustice and inequality in just about every category of women's lives more obvious and more alarming than ever. But sadly, that doesn't necessarily mean we're going to change in response.

The pandemic provided women who ordinarily enjoyed the freedom and confidence that comes from leaving the house to work the chance to do the laundry while they were on a conference call. So many of us found ourselves working from home during lockdown, which was great for being able to sneak in a quick online Pilates session at lunch, but also blurred the boundaries between our personal lives and professional obligations. Writer Gideon Haigh has explored how the pandemic has shifted our relationship with the office, saying that the success of working from home has reminded workers of the importance of privacy in a workplace. 'People suddenly in their home got back a bit of privacy. They actually got the opportunity to do some uninterrupted work,' says Haigh. He argues that if working in offices continue into the future, employers will need to be cognisant of this and 'come up with a means by which the workplaces that we have are geared to those parts of work that are generally collaborative.'

While the shift to online technologies and working from home has been beneficial for many employees, Haigh tells me that working women are at a disadvantage.[58] 'Dad is always busy with his stuff. He's just that much harder to interrupt, whereas Mum is always more accessible and the person to whom children turn. Women are significantly disadvantaged in an ongoing sense from the move towards working from home,' says Haigh. He believes that working from home has greater benefits for employers than employees. 'They're basically getting another two hours of work out of us. That commute that we took at the start of the top of the day; that hasn't become our time, that's become their time. People are working longer and more arduously and they're consoling themselves with the idea that they're doing it in their pyjamas, but they're working.' If this is the future of work, women will likely be working longer and harder while also still taking on the burden of unpaid labour. The consequences of this started to reveal themselves during Covid-19, with many women reporting feeling more stretched between their ever-expanding list of responsibilities. The pandemic is making us rethink the way our work lives operate. Whether that will ultimately be a good thing for women remains to be seen.

If women in two-parent households were doing it tough, the struggle for women in single-parent families was even harder. The majority of single-parent households in Australia are women, with data from the Australian Bureau of Statistics estimating that they make up 81 per cent of one-parent families.[59] Melbourne-based Karen Pickering is a single mum and sole carer of her child who lives with a disability, and she's pretty familiar with these challenges. Pickering says that taking over the professional care that couldn't be accessed during lockdown for her son added to her load. Without childcare to rely on, she had to work to support her family while simultaneously caring for her family. It felt nearly impossible. Nonetheless, Pickering tells me that she felt more supported financially during that time by the government than ever before. Pickering says that keeping welfare support payments below the poverty line ensures that more women and children end up scraping by each week. 'We should stop making single mothers pay for childcare and look at different kinds of government-mandated tax relief,' she says. Free childcare was, in fact, introduced by the federal government in April 2020, giving hundreds of thousands a short-term reprieve. This government-funded act was revolutionary and should be the norm. Childcare costs in

Australia are particularly high and limit the participation of women in the workforce. Freed from the mental balancing act of comparing their post-tax incomes with the cost of care, unemployed Australian women returned to work faster than their male counterparts. Sadly, the policy move was short-lived despite the positive economic and social impacts.

While the Australian government is to be applauded for its overall response to Covid-19 – stepping in to support the community financially, keeping us connected to work and keeping us safe – there were still gaps. In fact, there was sheer short-sightedness in a range of policy areas.

Amanda is an international student who works in aged care. The twenty-seven-year-old is pursuing a master's degree in social work and has been living in Australia for close to a decade. 'When the pandemic hit, I was due to finish a course I was studying in June 2020,' she tells me. 'But due to the pandemic, my course was put on hold, and I was basically in limbo.' Amanda tells me that she was angry international students weren't being adequately supported. 'I was really frustrated by the government. I do understand the concept of feeding your own first, however, I feel they had a duty of care to give at least more warning for people who were not citizens to leave the country,' she says. Amanda believes other countries did a better job at supporting people on visas. 'Watching our counterparts in New Zealand where the Prime Minister Jacinda Ardern said that the whole country is going into lockdown. If you have a visa, don't worry about it. Immigration will take care of it. We'll extend everyone's visas. Seeing other countries doing that and then being in Australia where you're on your own. Sink or swim; you decided to come here, figure yourself out.'

The uncertainty took a toll on Amanda's mental health. 'Just not knowing what would happen to me and fearing for my health, having to work in aged care and disability was quite a challenge,' she says. Despite these challenges, as a frontline worker, Amanda considered herself one of the lucky ones. 'I had the means to survive. I really felt discouraged and upset and sad for other international students who didn't have the means to survive.' About half a million international students were in Australia when the pandemic began. They were left without access to welfare support, to Medicare or to JobKeeper. Many had their jobs cancelled. The remainder could generally not afford the exorbitant cost of flights home and others did not want to leave the country they had called home for so many years. It was proof that personal connection to a community and a place goes beyond a piece of paper with 'Citizenship' written across the top. With international education contributing more than $40 billion to the Australian economy in 2019,[60] you would have thought our leaders could extend a little more generosity during a global crisis. Apparently, the cost of compassion was higher than we had thought.

For some women, non-binary people and children, home was the most dangerous place for them to be during Covid-19. Hannah* is a single mum of one who had been in a long-distance relationship with her abusive partner Alan* for several years. 'It was what I thought was a really nice relationship for a long period of time,' she told me. 'But I guess that's because in a long-distance relationship, you get to see the highlights of people's lives rather than how they actually live. Looking back now, the start of some of the warning signs were there prior to me moving, but I just attributed it to the fact that we were in a long-distance relationship.' Hannah says that the signs were 'very much around possessiveness of time and location and if I wasn't available to talk to Alan when he was driving home from work, he got very angry and annoyed. I felt increasingly like I had to be available whenever he called.' Hannah says that Alan began requesting daily photographs of her so he could 'see what I was wearing or what I looked like'. Initially, Hannah found this behaviour to be 'kinda cutesy' but then it became more controlling. Soon, she was required to check in and report on how she styled her hair, what clothes she was wearing and whether or not she had make-up on.

Hannah decided to take a chance on the relationship and relocated interstate to be closer to Alan. It was then that the controlling behaviour escalated. Alan had asked her to move in with him, but Hannah rejected the request. It didn't take long for the physical abuse to start. Hannah had only been in town for nine days at the time and she vividly recalls the incident. 'It was my birthday. Alan locked me in a room and told me to call Relationships Australia and talk to them about what I was doing wrong in the relationship and that I'd driven him to that. He said that it was my fault,' she recounts. 'I started to modify my behaviour to please him. If I displeased Alan, or did something he didn't like, then he would ignore me for days and then I would have to come back and apologise.' Although Hannah wasn't living with her perpetrator when the nationwide lockdown measures came into effect, it was a terrifying time. Border closures meant that she was isolated in a new city and didn't know anyone but Alan. 'Things started to escalate more the longer that I was here because I wasn't allowed to have friends,' says Hannah. 'I was very isolated. I didn't have anywhere to turn.' It didn't help that the working-from-home environment made it difficult to confide in her colleagues. 'At home, I was not around anyone. If anything happened, there was no one to check on me or to make sure I was okay.' Women like Hannah often remain in dangerous situations because they're not supported adequately by governments. When governments cut funds for domestic abuse services and women's refuges, there is less support available for the scarily large number of women who need it.

If the victim-survivors of domestic abuse were in a precarious position before 2020, the pandemic only made it worse. Underlying the pandemic, Australia has got a continuing epidemic of violence against women and girls. This is true despite the millions of dollars being pumped into public awareness campaigns aimed at shifting community attitudes. Both state and federal governments committed to doing more but so far, nothing is shifting the terrifying reality that more than one woman a week is killed by her current or former intimate partner. A group calling itself Destroy the Joint[61] keeps a tally of the number of women who are killed by violence in Australia every year, a grim count of the mothers, sisters, aunts, daughters and friends murdered by men. While Covid-19 restrictions were enforced to protect people from one danger, they left many women more acutely exposed to another. According to the United Nations women's agency UN Women, prior to the pandemic, 1 in 3 women experienced intimate or sexual violence mostly by an intimate partner.[62] The agency reported a global surge in cases following Covid-19.

Chief Executive of Women's Safety NSW Hayley Foster tells me that in her line of work, 'we had the worst year we had seen in our working memories'. The pandemic highlighted to Foster how old methods of support were ineffective in supporting women. 'There was a lack of availability of face-to-face services, and accommodation support and people were not feeling safe to go out and access support accommodation,' she says. For many women who were in abusive relationships, there was a clear lack of accessible options for them to safely leave. 'We had a lot of victim-survivors who were saying, "I want to leave, I'm terrified. But at the same time, I'm also terrified of catching Covid by moving my kids into a refuge",' says Foster. Unsurprisingly, women put the needs of their families above their own. 'Often, the women in the family will be prioritising just keeping the family together – just keeping everything going,' explains Foster. 'Just trying to keep food on the table and roofs over everyone's heads at that time and really don't prioritise their own safety. We had a lot more strangulations, a lot more threats on people's lives and their children's lives, a lot more use of weapons, a lot more sexual assaults during the pandemic.'

A survey by the Australian Institute of Criminology[63] asked 15 000 women about their experience of domestic abuse during the initial stages of the pandemic. They ended up with a list of alarming but unsurprising factors that made these victim-survivors feel even more unsafe than usual. They were spending more time with their abusers, for one, and less able to escape to places where they felt safe or could ask for help. These women were more socially isolated than ever, with restricted movement outside of the home. They felt they had fewer options for assistance and support. Many were beholden financially to their abusers, which limited or decimated their chances of leaving. On top of all that, the insecurity of a global pandemic made a lot of abusers feel out of control, which we know often makes them angrier, more violent and more dangerous. As ever, women from marginalised backgrounds have been particularly vulnerable. Aboriginal and Torres Strait Islander women are the most at-risk group for experiencing domestic and family violence in Australia, with estimates that they are between two and five times more likely to experience violence compared to non-Indigenous women. A report conducted by Women's Safety NSW[64] found an increase in the number of reported domestic violence cases by Indigenous women and concluded they were at risk of experiencing violence at high levels of severity. Contributing factors to the increased risk included the inability to attend cultural support groups and women prioritising basic needs over safety. The report's authors identified service gaps for Indigenous women and children having access to support for complex needs and ongoing accommodation.

Women from migrant and refugee backgrounds were also at risk of experiencing domestic violence at higher rates during the pandemic. According to InTouch, a Victorian specialist family violence organisation, women on temporary visas experienced further hardship and marginalisation.[65] InTouch says that many women temporary visa holders were excluded from the government's JobKeeper program, and many were already ineligible for JobSeeker, with some without working rights. Where they did work, it was generally in casualised industries that were severely impacted by public health measures, including the beauty and hospitality industries. This meant that many migrant and refugee women subsequently lost their jobs, leaving them particularly vulnerable.

While early predictions during Covid-19 forecast an increase in women accessing domestic violence helplines, and while according to UN Women this did increase five-fold in some countries,[66] here in Australia, there was an initial decline.[67] Hayley Foster corroborates this. 'We didn't necessarily see a huge increase in calls to our support services until lockdown restrictions were lifting.' This was likely because it was unsafe for women to call for help while they shared such close and constant quarters with their abusers. This surveillance also manifested in other ways. There was a reported increase in so-called technology-facilitated abuse. This includes stalking victims online, abusive messages or calls, being tracked through phones or devices, accessing the victim's online accounts and creating fake social media accounts to harass and abuse victims. According to a report by Women's Services Network,[68] which has been tracking technological abuse since 2015, it saw a 244.8 per cent increase in respondents seeing perpetrators use GPS for tracking of victim-survivors, a 114.9 per cent increase in the use of text messages, emails and instant messaging to surveil women, and a 183.2 per cent increase in the use of video cameras, which create a climate of intense monitoring and surveillance. Without changes to legislation that criminalises this behaviour, this is likely to continue post Covid-19.

Hannah has survived all of this. She says that Alan regularly hacked her accounts and monitored her online behaviour. She had no privacy and no avenues to ask for help. She was literally trapped at home, with all of her lifelines to the outside world being inspected daily. 'I knew he was hacking into my stuff,' she tells me. 'But I couldn't prove that it was him. I would see that alt-right stuff was coming up that I had never searched for. Or I could see a profile on Tinder that I never put on there.' Hannah's experience highlights one of the crucial challenges in the current system for victim-survivors of domestic abuse – the enormous and often insurmountable burden of proof that lies with them. Women are statistically extremely unlikely to lie about abuse, and yet so many are disbelieved, dismissed and failed by a woeful system that's disgracefully committed to putting the freedom of men above the safety of women. After all that Hannah went through, she still didn't feel prepared to report her abuser, in part because she knew how her own actions would be interpreted. 'I didn't go to the police with bruises around my neck the day after he tried to strangle me,' she says. 'I hid it. I actively hid it. I put a scarf around my neck, and I didn't tell anyone because it was my fault. And by the time I went to the police, there was no proof.' Alan has not been convicted because of the absence of admissible evidence in court.

I despair. How is it that we are we still making justice and safety so difficult for women in this country, even more so during a pandemic? Women like Hannah are still not being believed even though they are being manipulated, emotionally controlled and physically confined. Professor Marilyn McMahon is the deputy dean of Deakin University's School of Law and has researched coercive control legislation both in Australia and overseas. Speaking to *ABC News*, Dr McMahon says coercive control is a major pattern of behaviour prior to homicide.[69] 'It is really disturbing that the biggest predictor of intimate partner homicide – the biggest risk factor – is not a previous history of physical violence within the relationship but a history of coercive controlling behaviour,' she says. With an absence of legislation that criminalises these behaviours, it's difficult to see how things for women like Hannah will improve.

Women continue to be killed. How many dead women will it take, or women raped and assaulted, before we stop asking them to debate and defend their humanity? When will we simply listen to them? What will it take to fully acknowledge that most domestic violence is carried out by men and that the failure to name this correctly contributes to our inability to recognise, understand, and prevent it? It is male violence that women are demanding safety from, and Australia is unwilling to give it to them.

In the absence of legal reforms, perhaps coming up with new ways to help and protect women, particularly during a pandemic, might be a way forward. In Europe, victims of domestic abuse could use code words at the pharmacy to summon police help during lockdown. In January 2021, the British government launched an initiative called the Ask for ANI (Action Needed Immediately) scheme,[70] which allows those at risk or experiencing abuse to discreetly signal that they need help and access support at a pharmacy, one of the few essential businesses allowed to remain open during the lockdowns. The code-word scheme allows victims access to trained staff and provides a safe space for victims to ask for help if they were unable to access help elsewhere. A similar model is on the cards here in Australia, thanks to family violence advocacy group Safe Steps. According to the group's proposal,[71] secure spaces and phone access to call police or other services would be provided by trained supermarket staff. This is encouraging because should we live through another pandemic, supermarkets will remain open and are one of the few public spaces that women can go to alone. Hopefully, more of these smart systems will be established in the wake of the pandemic. After a uniquely horrifying time for women, please, let's take the chance to reimagine a better and safer society for all of us.

When politicians let women down, ordinary citizens often step up in their place. In the absence of government assistance, communities came together during the pandemic to support women experiencing domestic abuse. Remember InTouch, the Victorian-based specialist family violence organisation providing support to women from migrant and refugee backgrounds that I mentioned earlier? Well, they partnered with social enterprises like Sibling Kinfolk to provide emergency food relief to women who were ineligible for social benefits because of their visa status. Every week, Victorians donated to this program to support some of the most vulnerable in the community. While it frustrates me that local people have to mobilise around women to find them adequate support, the reality is that grassroots responses like these do work. People like Diana Sayed and her team have the connection, language, and cultural understanding to provide access for some women that mainstream services may not.

Such options are often more effective than government-imposed solutions because they are closer to the community members and can respond to specific and unique needs. Diana Sayed says that any long-term solutions from government recognise the benefits of individualised community services. She also wants intersectionality embedded in any policy reform. 'I would like to see the specialised family violence organisations and the specialist multicultural communities empowered on a longer-term basis to drive the change that is needed in their own communities,' she says. 'Not to go back to these mainstream organisations which are often run by white women and are often a top-down approach, which doesn't work for us. We need much more funding at the community grassroots level. That's where the organising happens. That's where the change happens.' Clearly, local women know and have solutions to many of these issues. They stepped up when government supports were stretched thin during the pandemic. Imagine what they could achieve if given both ongoing funding *and* autonomy.

Jaanvi* works in an independent supermarket in regional Victoria. She is also an Uber driver in the bigger regional cities and towns along the coastline. On the weekends, she bulk cooks food for wealthy families who don't have the time or skill to make curries for themselves. And she does all this with four children aged between five and fourteen. Jaanvi doesn't complain. After migrating to Australia seventeen years ago as a newlywed, she has permanent residency and the social support of the government. 'I am grateful that we have come here,' she explains. 'India is ravaged by the Covid. Every day, I call or email to see how my family and friends are doing and it is not good. They are coughing from all the smoke of the burning funeral pyres. They wear masks but it cannot do much when nobody can get the vaccinations.'

During the pandemic, Jaanvi kept going to work. When Uber shifts slowed down because nobody was going anywhere, she set herself up on AirTasker and became inundated with work. She would collect people's washing from their doorstep before going to work at the supermarket. She would wash and dry it overnight before returning it the next morning. These were the very same nights she was bulk cooking more food than ever for people stuck at home. Presumably because those people could no longer go out to restaurants or were so overburdened with additional responsibilities that they needed respite from cooking. 'I was happy to have this work,' Jaanvi says. 'Not everyone had a job during the Covid and with no Uber to drive, I was very worried about where we would get money. Supermarket work does not pay well and also made me very scared. I liked to see our customers because they were very talkative during the Covid. Mostly people were not rude to me because we live in a small place. It was nice to see them, but I was scared to catch the virus and take it home to my children.' Jaanvi's children did not have the benefit of a parent whose job allowed them to homeschool. They went to school when the government allowed it but otherwise, they took care of themselves. With two working parents who were deemed essential to the community during the pandemic, they were pretty much on their own. Jaanvi is upfront about this because she knows there wasn't another choice. 'If you have to decide between sitting with them while they do their games or going to work and paying for their food? You go to work and you pay for their food.' Jaanvi is like so many migrant and disadvantaged women around Australia who did it tough in the pandemic, scrambling to make ends meet without complaint. Her work was something the community could not afford to go without, yet she was paid so little for it, she had to do multiple odd jobs on the side, leaving her only snatches of time to rest and be with her family. What does this mean for a person's physical and mental health? Not just in the immediate moment, but into the long term?

The much-repeated catchcry of political leaders, commentators, celebrities and influencers when raising public health awareness about the pandemic was 'Stay home. Save lives'.[72] I heard the Victorian Premier repeat this slogan every time he'd address a daily press conference. While I do not doubt the importance of this messaging, it did get me thinking about the people who simply couldn't afford to stay home, and whether the way we spoke about these people was in a loving way. The United Nations Special Rapporteur on Human Rights Phillip Alston agreed.[73] He described these sort of directives as a 'moral failing of epic proportions'. The pandemic, according to Alston 'disproportionately affects poor people, who are more likely to have health complications, live in crowded housing, lack the resources to stay at home for long periods, and work low-paid jobs that force them to choose between risking their health or losing their income.' The data also shows that women are disproportionately represented in these categories, and an unintended consequence was the so-called 'pandemic shaming' that resulted from this all-or-nothing messaging. At a time when mental health was having a severe impact on people's wellbeing, adding more shame to the plates of people already burdened with the responsibilities of surviving during a pandemic seemed cruel. Hashtags like #covidiot and images of people who appeared not to be observing the guidelines spread like a bushfire. Going out to work because you needed money to survive was seen as putting lives at risk rather than recognised as a necessary act to keep your own life financially viable. While Jaanvi was spared the abuse reported by many low-income essential workers – or she chose not to disclose it – many weren't. There was shame in not having a well-paid office job that could relatively easily be done at home. The fact is, while it's easy to generalise and paint people with the same judgemental brush, the reasons why some people didn't adhere to the directives are complicated and varied. Do the complications of class and race offend the fabled Australian commitment to egalitarianism? Perhaps that is why we can't bring ourselves to reckon properly with the fact that there are individuals who are scraping out a living with no choice but to go to work during a pandemic, even if it means breaking the law.

This is not to excuse irresponsible behaviour, but perhaps in the aftermath of the pandemic, it's worth considering *how* we talk to people when communicating public messages and to not make assumptions about why some people might not adhere to them. The government is fond of reminding us that we're all in the same boat. But we're not. We're all caught in the same storm but some people's boats are simply fancier and more buoyant than others.

American writer and academic Dr Cornel West once said that justice is what love looks like in public, just like tenderness is what love feels like in private. At the core of feminism is justice. It is a justice that is intertwined with economic justice, racial justice, climate justice, all types of justice. Women already have the solutions for many of the challenges that confront us – report after report makes countless recommendations and little, if any, are implemented. And so the cycle continues. I hope that this moment in time presents an opportunity for those in positions of power to start listening – not passively, but actively listening and engaging with the research seeking to bridge the gender inequality gap. Women know what the problems are and how to fix them, and it's time for those in positions of power to support those organisations that have been doing the work. Whether it's organisations supporting and working with Indigenous women, women from migrant and refugee backgrounds, or single mothers – they know what and how change needs to happen. All they are missing is the means.

Caring for women in the aftermath of the pandemic means recognising the vital role that unpaid labour contributes to our economies. Covid exposed how much of the formal economy depends on the subsidised labour predominantly undertaken by women. And this, of course, has implications for our relationships. The redistribution of labour equitably within the home is one way of working towards gender equality in those spaces. There were encouraging signs of a cultural shift, with early data here in Australia revealing that men were taking on more care and domestic work in the home, providing an opportunity to change these gendered norms. Covid-19 was regarded as the great equaliser and in some ways, it has been. We have each been exposed to the hidden lives of other family members which we perhaps were less aware of before. Nonetheless, lockdowns did not expose us to the lived experience of everyone, just those in our immediate proximity.

It's impossible to talk about how we love post-pandemic without addressing the social, political and economic failures that contribute to, and limit, our capacity to care for not just those in our immediate circles, but in our communities and elsewhere. We know that the pandemic adversely impacted already marginalised people. The poor got poorer, the job-insecure became jobless, the lonely became quite literally alone and the abused became frightened for their very existence. Any meaningful solutions cannot avoid or ignore intersectionality. The complex and intersecting identities of women and non-binary people cannot be seen through a singular lens – the unwillingness to do so will further entrench gender inequality.

Women did not have a singular experience during the pandemic. Some women were fine and others struggled to stay afloat and alive. The data repeatedly shows that Indigenous women, women from migrant and refugee backgrounds, single parents, women from low socio-economic backgrounds and disabled women were disproportionately affected because of entrenched social and economic marginalisation. If we weren't talking about intersectionality before, we can't avoid it in its aftermath. The pandemic has blown wide open the marginalisation that exists when characteristics such as gender, race and class overlap and intersect.

There are entrenched economic realities that need to shift, yes, but as a community we also need to be more empathetic and respectful. We should be listening to Indigenous women, women who have inherited such vast wisdom. First Nations communities were the most successful in containing the pandemic even though they were most at risk from the virus. This is not a small feat. There was much to learn from their triumph, yet we barely saw mention of this in the media or on those endless Zoom calls. According to the Aboriginal and Torres Strait Islander Social Justice Commissioner June Oscar, Indigenous communities kept Covid-19 infection rates six times lower than the rest of Australia without a single death.

Writing in the 2021 Closing The Gap report,[74] Oscar said this was further evidence that Aboriginal and Torres Strait Islander people having control over their own lives guarantees success. 'As we have all said, time and again, we know what is best for our own health and wellbeing, and that of our families and wider communities. When control is in our hands, when we can exercise autonomy, we succeed.' Policymaking that is led by those at the centre of its impact is not just a warm hug and cup of cocoa approach to governing – it is meaningful and effective. There is knowledge that can only be borne of firsthand experience. Professor Jaky Troy tells me that some of that success could be attributed to Aboriginal and Torres Strait Islander women who, in many instances, led the outreach and the information sharing as well as checking in on members of the community and ensuring that elders were protected and looked after. If only we allocated adequate resources to communities and afforded them the autonomy to find their own solutions.

How do we talk about love without talking about the structural barriers that limit our capacity to love ourselves and those around us? There's a misplaced and false argument that's trotted out by mainstream feminists claiming that achieving gender equality is a matter of personal psychology. You know, that workplace and career success are as simple as just leaning in, ladies. Well, not quite. It's a lot more complicated when you add the additional discrimination women face because of race, religion, sexuality or disability. Can these women break free by simply 'leaning in'? I don't think so. Can women who work in frontline, insecure, underpaid jobs break free by simply 'leaning in'? The evidence in front of us shows otherwise. This myth that women should change their behaviour to get the outcome they desire, when the reality is that structural barriers inhibit women from doing so, is a damaging one. It is one that pulls us apart from one another rather than using whatever privilege we have to lift up the voices of other women. It's a trope that shows up when women are sexually abused or assaulted and the blame is shifted on to them. It shows up again when single mothers are mocked and shamed because of societal attitudes. It shows up even more during a global pandemic and, unfortunately, will only get worse from here if we allow it to fester.

When the second lockdown in Victoria was lifted, I tried to carry some of the lessons from lockdown into the world as I re-emerged. But I'll be honest, I quickly defaulted to old patterns of behaviour until I realised that words mean nothing without action. And action requires courage. The fact is, a gender-equitable future requires each one of us courageously choosing to act from a place of love, even if it goes against our own self-interest in the short-term. This is easier said than done, I know. But the alternative, doing nothing and continuing to move through life as we did prior to the pandemic, will entrench inequality. The pandemic showed us what can happen when we show up for each other – whether it's our neighbours or friends we haven't caught up with in years – and the impact this has on the community. *Love.*

Grief, a shared ritual, was disrupted and the cumulative impact of it on our communities will be devastating if strategies, like those proposed in Canada, aren't put in place. Recognising that the road out of this pandemic will be long and will impact each one of us differently, and pre-emptively putting in measures that ensure people are supported, including culturally appropriate services, will help us to feel less alone. *Love.*

Taking the time to slow down and be patient with each other in our friendships and relationships was another lesson this past year taught me. Covid highlighted how much we value social connections and the loss of these has significant consequences on our wellbeing. *Love.*

To love beyond the sentimental takes courage. After a year in which we all experienced pain and loss at some level, the biggest lesson I've learned is that suffering is absolute. I may not be able to relate to Chloé's experience of parenting during lockdown, or directly go through what Hannah did, surviving an abusive relationship. Nor was I caring for a child on my own like Karen, or navigating the complexities of living in Australia on a visa with little government support, like Amanda. I did not work four jobs that all required me to endanger my life by leaving the house like Jaanvi, and I didn't watch my mother die on a Zoom call like Monica. There are pains and injustices of the most personal parts of women's lives that have been carried by sisters all over Australia, not to mention beyond its shores. But while none of these women's stories were my own, I believe we will not move forward until women see one another's struggles as theirs. We don't need to experience the pain to know that these women suffered and continue to suffer – what we need to do is ensure that women feel supported when they experience these struggles. Having empathy allows us to lobby for the systemic change that's required, because that's love.

Until we collectivise the experience of womanhood such that the suffering or disadvantage or abuse of one is the plight of the whole, until we protect every woman in Australia, we're protecting none of them. Any one of us could end up in situations that we couldn't imagine. At every turn, women remain worse off. Our collective responsibility is not to be dismissive of each other's pain and suffering, but instead to hold space for each other. And instead of thinking, 'that couldn't be me', it's seeing ourselves in these experiences – regardless of what some male politicians would have us believe. These women are our friends, our sisters, our daughters, our nieces, our grandmothers, our colleagues – they are us. Caring for another woman isn't conditional on the fact that I am a woman – I just happen to be a woman who wants to live in a world that treats everyone equitably. Love means centring the voices of those who have been historically marginalised and respectfully finding a way of reimagining our shared futures. Love means worrying about the child next door as much as your own, yes, but it also means worrying about the child of colour four suburbs away, and the disabled child at the local school just as much. It means worrying about a child living in poverty, and a child whose mother is being beaten each night when she 'stays home to stay safe'. Love means valuing each person, recognising their particular experience – and finding ways within our own communities to help.

The pandemic forced us to prioritise what mattered most to us. Whether it was leaving the job or relationships that no longer served us, spending more time caring for elderly parents and with our children, for many of us, we weren't willing to put off these things any longer. These invaluable lessons are worth holding on to in the aftermath of the pandemic as we rebuild and restructure our lives. The realisation that to thrive, we need to be supported by our friends and families, but that support from institutions and governments is just as – if not more – vital. When governments offered financial support and relief to Australian families during the pandemic, there was a lot of evidence that showed that this went a long way in people being able to cope during uncertain times and we know that uncertainty impacts our relationships with ourselves and those around us. There's little time to think about ovaries and dating when you're worried you might lose your job. These measures shouldn't only exist in times of crisis – the pandemic has shown that we are capable of caring for each other.

While a shift in cultural attitudes is vital, much of the heavy lifting should not and cannot be left to individuals. The burden of making the ethical and moral choices on complex policy matters creates a culture of shaming and judgement when the reality is, most people are trying their best with the cards they've been dealt. Every person's circumstance is unique to them. Shaming a mum for not being able to bake after school with their kids, or judging women who choose to be childfree, or the guilt that ensues because women feel the societal pressure of not being the 'perfect parent' – these emotions keep us punching down, attacking each other and ourselves when, really, we should be punching up.

Addressing gender injustice requires fundamental changes that can only be solved through political institutions and leadership. Collectively, we need political will and strong leadership to solve the problems of gender inequality. Individually, we can be responsible for ukukhapha – showing up for each other beyond catchy slogans and shareable Instagram captions. It means advocating for policy changes that ensure no woman is left behind in this country, whether it's signing a petition, calling a local MP, showing up to a rally, or donating to or volunteering with an organisation that supports women. Any hopes of dismantling gender inequality in the future will require each of us in our own corners of the country to roll up our sleeves and show up for each other – that is love in action.

During the pandemic, I moved into a new apartment building. Unlike in the past, when I hardly knew the names of my neighbours, I decided to make the effort to know the people who lived closest to me. It has taken a bit of getting used to the small talk, but it has changed my life for the better.

The pandemic coaxed me into valuing friendship and companionship more than ever, even with strangers and neighbours and colleagues. I regularly meet with the people in my building to socialise – an unexpected joy after a year of isolation. My single friends and I regularly check in on each other; this weekly ritual, or 'pulse check' as I call it, has been a comforting reminder that even during a health and economic crisis, I am not alone – and I never have been.

Body.

Emily J. Brooks

Emily J. Brooks is a writer and editor. Formerly, she was the editor of Future Women, an organisation dedicated to the advancement of women. She was also an associate editor at *The Huffington Post Australia* and a journalist at *The Australian Women's Weekly*. Emily's work has appeared in *Grazia*, *The Sydney Morning Herald*, and *The Age*, among other places.

The beginning of lockdown resembled a sort of apocalyptic retreat. After the fridge was stocked with fresh food and the cupboards filled with cans, I fled the safety of my home, once more, for Aesop. I returned with an $83 serum that defied all rationality but delivered a purpose. I would end March of 2020 with a clean face and a sense of order.

There were no dinners to attend or plans to cancel. The world had cancelled everything and I was quietly thrilled. I'd been granted the one thing I had always wanted more of – time – and revelled in the question of what to do with it. I would develop a significant yoga habit and meditate twice daily. I would organise my emails and declutter my apartment. It would be a process of reduction, not accumulation, and I wasn't just talking about furniture here. I wasn't going to live the busy, frantic life I'd been living; one with contending priorities and an overwhelming to-do list. I was going to live slower, simpler, and re-emerge from this pandemic as *her*. The woman who did yoga every morning and owned an inbox that frequently returned to zero – and always fit into her jeans.

When I was having these thoughts, I lived in a one-bedroom apartment that overlooked an empty beach in the eastern suburbs of Sydney. It was so strange seeing the normally busy-to-bursting blanket of sand devoid of people. My boyfriend joked that we lived above a national park. The long stretch of white sand reflected the expansiveness of my mood and the possibility of fresh starts. I was a twenty-eight-year-old writer who had just taken the plunge – the risk – to go freelance. My first book was being released later in the year. As the world was shutting down, I was starting a new chapter. I had the privilege of good health, no dependants, and a safe home to retreat to. Although, if I'm honest with you, I wasn't without fear. I didn't have the economic security of a full-time job during the biggest global health crisis of my lifetime. The timing of my decision to go freelance was completely laughable, because if you didn't laugh, you'd cry. So, I silenced that fear often and focused on the silver linings. I had book edits and an empty calendar, which felt like something closer to a gift. I was stuck in a tiny one-bedroom apartment and for the first time in a long time, I felt like I had space.

I know I wasn't alone here.

The pandemic has embodied countless paradoxes – the enemy is invisible, the greatest way to help is by doing nothing at all – and this was just another. Government-mandated time inside gifted me the reflective pause I needed. My own desires to become a better version of myself were cast against a backdrop of mass human suffering. The novel slowness of my days were juxtaposed with images of mass graves on Hart Island, New York, and Italian military vehicles transporting bodies. I carried grief for those suffering and hope for individual self-improvement while simultaneously punishing myself for what felt like shameful introspection. I doused my face with expensive serum before bed only to lay there, awake.

The philosopher Alain de Botton once said that humans are ordering animals. Everything we contribute to, be it literature, science or politics, is an attempt to create a sense of order in the chaos. I guess that is what was happening here. As a global health crisis wreaked havoc across the world, I tried to create a long stretch of white sand in my mind. A private beach filled with fitness routines and cleared inboxes and well-fitted jeans and control. It was a delusional, selfish act but it was also an attempt to create a sense of order in the chaos. I couldn't control the growing death toll that I checked a stupid amount of times each night, but I could control my little world. Other people controlled their worlds too. They enthusiastically embraced sourdough starters and ticked off long-neglected jobs around the house. They put puzzles back together and planted new gardens and embraced virtual workouts like it was their sole purpose in life.

We weren't frontline workers bearing the emotional and physical cost of this pandemic, but citizens following stay-at-home orders. The solitude we were asked to embrace soon became a condition many of us wanted to live with in a more ongoing way. The pause reprogrammed us. When everything was cancelled, when our days were stripped of the superfluous, our priorities rearranged themselves and suddenly became clearer. The composer and music producer Quincy Jones once said that all you need in this life is love to share, health to spare, and friends who care. Our post-pandemic priorities feel a little like that. People are moving out of big cities to find more space and slow down. Others are hiking more and joining open swimming groups. Some have grown to enjoy their reduced work hours and are spending more time with their families. Many of us are socialising less than we were before the pandemic started but are more present for the conversations in front of us.

This pandemic has been a time of mass human suffering, but it has also given way to something that feels like a new way of living. The question now is whether it can maintain its hold.

In the Infectious Disease Unit of the Royal Adelaide Hospital, Anna Liptak, forty-six, was lying in a cream room with dark thoughts. She had just been diagnosed with severe Covid, which is something around 20 per cent of Covid-19 patients endure. Anna had spent the past week struggling to breathe. Just one day before, she'd been at home with what she thought was sinusitis. Now, doctors and nurses would spend thirty minutes putting on protective clothing before they could even be in the same room as her. Usually, Anna lives her life outdoors. She's a personal trainer, who helps hundreds of her clients get fitter and healthier. It made no sense to her why she would be one of the first people in South Australia to be diagnosed with Covid-19. Anna had run twenty-seven marathons. She was fit, healthy and middle-aged. She wasn't immunocompromised. But as she lay there, alone, all Anna could think about were the people she *had* compromised.

One week earlier, Anna had attended a conference, where she and a colleague had been trying to sell a fitness documentary. She returned home with a headache and the next day collapsed on the laundry floor. Her GP diagnosed her with the abovementioned sinusitis, but there was something in the back of her mind telling her it was more. She was bedridden, struggling to breathe, occasionally attempting to return to regularity. There had been one comparatively good day when Anna had felt a little better and deluded herself into running one of her scheduled fitness classes. She'd do anything to take it back. One of Anna's fitness class clients had a husband with lung cancer. If he contracted the virus because of Anna, he might die. If that happened, she would never forgive herself.

Anna turned on the TV from her hospital bed and reeled at the images on the news from overseas. Italy, America, Spain. Mothers, daughters, fathers, sons. There was a woman in the US who had passed the virus onto her mother and her mother had died. Anna had seen her mother just recently. What if she died? Or her father? What if her husband had Covid? Or her teenage children?

The phone rang. Anna's sixteen-year-old son, Zach, had Covid-19. Anna spent the next three days worrying about everyone but herself. Meanwhile, her husband was riddled with anxiety, dressing in PPE to scrub their family home from top to bottom. The couple's fourteen-year-old son, Lachy, was isolated in one room while Zach was isolated in another. Anna controlled what she could through her phone. Zach's condition wasn't critical, so Anna had pleaded with doctors to let him isolate at home. 'He wouldn't be able to cope in here,' she told them. Researchers in China have found that 96.2 per cent of clinically stable Covid-19 patients suffered from significant post-traumatic stress symptoms prior to discharge.[75] These symptoms, the researchers said, can potentially lead to negative long-term outcomes such as 'lower quality of life and impaired working performance'.

As Anna lay in her slim single bed, alone in hospital, she wondered how her family would fare.

After one week in the Infectious Disease Unit, Anna went home. Her health had improved, and she had convinced the doctors to allow her to isolate in her own bed. Her husband and youngest son moved to the family's holiday house, about an hour's drive away. She and Zach would stay isolated. An ambulance chaperoned her home. The sun was out and Anna lay by the pool with Zach. They couldn't physically do much but, guiltily, Anna didn't want this quiet, private time to end. They ordered Uber Eats. They chatted. They lay in silence with their eyes closed, basking in the sun like lizards. Life had been busy with two young kids and two businesses. In this strange stretch of suspended time, Anna could breathe and take it all in.

Cleaning the house gave Anna a sense of purpose. She had never been obsessed with cleanliness, but after being in hospital, she 'became obsessive very quickly'. As one of the early Covid-19 patients, Anna had felt 'diseased' and became fixated on staying clean. Psychologists believe obsessive-compulsive disorder, a manifestation of anxiety, could be one of the most prominent longer-term mental health issues to come from the pandemic. Author of *The Psychology of Pandemics,*[76] and a professor in psychiatry at the University of British Columbia, Steven Taylor believes the stress of the coronavirus is likely to trigger or worsen OCD in people who have a genetic predisposition towards forms of it, such as cleaning compulsions or contamination obsessions. Taylor told the BBC that unless people receive proper mental health treatment, they will become 'chronic germaphobes'.[77]

Nurses checked in on Anna and Zach every day. Her friends visited the family home and laid out a picnic on the front lawn. Zach and Anna sat inside, separated by a window. Someone pulled out an acoustic guitar and they all sang. Two weeks of horror were followed by overwhelming kindness and generosity. The all-clear came ten days after her discharge from hospital and by that time, Anna didn't want to leave the warm glow of her house. Adelaide is a small place and the family's story had been in the newspaper. Her friends may have sung to her but Anna had also received messages of abuse from strangers who blamed her for her own illness. The pandemic brought out the best and the worst in people.

Anna thought their world was the only one that stopped, but when she and Zach walked into the local shopping centre on their first excursion out of the house, it appeared that everyone else's had too. There were only a few stores open, so they walked into one. The shop assistant greeted them with a friendly hello and a fresh dose of gossip. 'Oh my god,' she said. 'Have you heard about the mother and son who have corona?' Zach looked at Anna, mortified. Anna and Zach returned to the car, then home, packed their bags, and drove an hour south to see the rest of their family. The four of them went for a surf and life felt good again. Almost normal. Privately vowing to slow down the pace of life and appreciate the small joys, Anna held on to her husband's hand while he looked at the water. He held it right back, nice and tight. When he did let go, he bent down and unconsciously washed the hand that had touched Anna's carefully in the ocean. It hurt, but Anna understood.

Women have been disproportionately impacted by the coronavirus. They have been far more likely to lose their jobs[78] during the pandemic and far more likely to carry the burden of caregiving responsibilities and unpaid work than men. This has clearly widened the economic gaps between women and men, but it has also caused a crisis in women's mental health. In September, the non-profit international aid organisation CARE released a study of 10 400 people from thirty-eight countries which revealed women are almost three times more likely to suffer from significant mental health issues than men. Nearly a third of women reported an increase in mental health challenges, compared to 10 per cent of men.[79] In Australia, the annual Jean Hailes Women's Health Survey revealed that one in three women are experiencing anxiety and one in four depression. This was highest in women aged between eighteen and twenty-five, with half feeling anxious and two-fifths depressed. Looking at the direct impact of the pandemic, more than 33 per cent of women reported that their overall health was worse.[80]

Suffering like this is impervious to privilege. In *Intimations*,[81] a book of essays released in 2020, Zadie Smith wrote that suffering is truly universal. 'Language, logic, argument, rationale and relative perspective itself are no match for it,' she wrote. 'Suffering applies itself directly to its subject and will not be shamed out of itself or eradicated by righteous argument, no matter how objectively correct that argument may be.' If it could, she wrote, the CEO's daughter wouldn't starve herself and the famous actor wouldn't take his own life. If it could, our suffering during the pandemic would be entirely suppressed by the knowledge that someone else's suffering was worse.

There have been radical differences in our pandemic experiences, but also an underlying sameness. We have been collectively isolated with the choices we made before the coronavirus arrived and left to grapple with them while it persisted. The single woman sitting alone in her apartment doesn't think anyone will ever know such loneliness. The mother trying to work while homeschooling three children is lonely without ever getting a moment alone. The junior doctor dressing in PPE each morning and spending each night alone with her trauma, unable to alleviate it with a beer at the pub with her colleagues. The manager of the aged care home and her residents banding together as they grapple with an outbreak. We've all suffered, to varying degrees, and have been in turns comforted and horrified by the commonality of the experience.

While it's never a good idea to engage in competitive grief, it's crucial to consider who fared worse than others during this unprecedented global crisis if we are to have any hope of coming out of it better than we came in.

Emma Fulu was crying in her car by lunchtime on the first day of formal homeschooling. She had escaped from her three children in order to have a breakdown in peace. She sat in the front seat, hands on the steering wheel, head in those hands, and howled. Life suddenly felt impossible. Her eldest son was nine years old, the twins were six, and they each wanted her attention at the same time, all the time. How was Emma supposed to tend to each child's individual education while also working? Impossible.

Emma is the founder of The Equality Institute, a global feminist agency working to advance gender equality and end violence against women and girls. She started the company in Melbourne after a decade working for the United Nations. When I spoke to Emma over the phone in November 2020, she had done a Pilates class and was in that delightful stage of post-exercise recovery where you need to be airlifted out of bed. It was the first class she'd done for eight months, which is a pretty good indication of both how thoroughly locked down Melbourne had been and how much time Emma had to look after herself recently.

Emma eloquently describes 2020 as 'a fucking nightmare'. She is a single parent and believes she was both better and worse off in different ways. She would have her children for one week, then her ex-husband would take them for the next, and back again. In the early days of the pandemic, Emma was enthusiastic. School holidays had been extended and she was getting creative with the kids while there were no formal lessons to worry about. They were making earrings and baking cupcakes together. Her focus was on keeping the three children in her home entertained. Then school holidays ended, and the homeschooling began. After her breakdown in the car, Emma began caring less and less about the schoolwork getting done. Hers became a mission of survival. While Emma was on Zoom calls with clients in other countries, her children would build Lego or watch TV. They would play quietly together and then play-fight and then actually fight, all while Emma kept her business ticking over and tended to the emotional needs of staff. The days began to blend into one another, and the nights were stolen by exhaustion. After a month of this awful cycle, Emma began to feel depressed.

According to Kaiser Family Foundation, an American non-profit that specialises in public health research,[82] the pandemic has exposed the deteriorating mental health of mothers who have been dealing with school closures, homeschool and a lack of childcare. Women with children are more likely to report symptoms of anxiety or depression than men with children; 49 per cent compared to 40 per cent. Emma had experienced one breakdown in her life prior to this and all the same signs began to emerge. She had regular nightmares. She broke out in acne. She was extremely emotional. She felt helpless. She visited her doctor for a mental health check and was diagnosed with burnout and situational depression. Single parents were allowed to put their children into childcare if they needed so eventually, Emma did. This reprieve lasted two weeks before the next school holidays began, and lockdown ended.

Then Melbourne's second wave arrived.

When stage four restrictions were enacted across the state, Emma was no longer allowed to put her kids into childcare. 'It nearly destroyed me,' she said. 'That's the thing with lockdown. These are not solvable problems. People were like, "What do you need?" And I'm like, "Well I need help, but I can't get it." So, at that time, there was no actual solution. I think that's what was sometimes so overwhelming. You feel trapped because you're like, "I know this is not working and I know what would help, but there's no way to get that help." And that's when you feel helpless.' Helplessness, like loneliness, became a familiar feeling during lockdowns around the world. You know how to help yourself, but you can't, and it's the knowing that leads to frustration and apathy. Our efforts to protect people from the physical effects of the virus by instigating things like quarantine created a secondary crisis of mental ill-health.

The term 'quarantine' was first used in Venice, Italy, in 1127 with regard to leprosy.[83] In the mid-1300s, it was widely used in response to the Black Death, a devastating global epidemic of bubonic plague that struck Europe and Asia. A review of literature[84] around quarantine shows that mental health continues to worsen as the duration of quarantine extends. When the second wave of the virus hit Melbourne, residents were forced into a lockdown that lasted 111 days. When the hotel quarantine program ended up causing more deaths, restrictions tightened even further. The state was moved into one of the strictest lockdowns in the world. It was meant to only last through August but was extended into September 2020. There were strict stay-at-home orders requiring residents to remain within 5 kilometres of their homes. Most businesses were closed and there was a nightly curfew. As *The New Yorker* wrote in January, 'For most people around the world, the stringency of the rules was hard to imagine.'

The negative psychological effects of quarantine include anger, confusion, and post-traumatic stress symptoms.

Spending more time in quarantine is a significant stressor, and some researchers have suggested there are long-lasting effects.[85] After stage four restrictions were announced, Lifeline saw a 30 per cent increase in calls from Victorians.[86] A week in to life under the restrictions, the Victorian government revealed there had been a 33 per cent increase in young people presenting to emergency departments due to self-harm compared to the same week in 2019.[87] Multiple studies conducted in Europe and China during the pandemic have linked post-traumatic stress symptoms with quarantines and lockdowns. A cross-sectional online survey conducted in Italy revealed that more than 29 per cent of respondents reported post-traumatic stress symptoms.[88] And another cross-sectional survey of more than 3400 people in Spain found that 18.6 per cent of respondents reported depressive symptoms, 21.6 per cent reported anxiety symptoms and 15.8 per cent reported PTSD symptoms.[89] Loneliness is the strongest predictor of depression, anxiety and PTSD.

A study of home-quarantined young people in China during the first month of the coronavirus outbreak revealed that 12.8 per cent of all participants had symptoms consistent with PTSD.[88] A longitudinal survey of almost 2000 people across 190 Chinese cities at the beginning of the outbreak, and again four weeks later, found that the majority of respondents were experiencing moderate to severe stress, anxiety and depression.[91] While research around the long-term mental health impacts of Melbourne's severe lockdown is still emerging, the Victorian healthcare system is continuing to deal with an onslaught of patients presenting with mental health problems – and this hasn't stopped since the state opened back up. Melbourne's gruelling lockdown, experts have argued, was a case of collective trauma, a traumatic event that was shared by a group of people. Well-known collective traumas include the Holocaust, American slavery, the Hiroshima and Nagasaki bombings, and September 11; but they can also include events such as a plane crash, war, famine, mass shootings, natural disasters or a pandemic. Collective trauma events can have direct and indirect impacts. In the case of this pandemic, the ramifications include health, employment and education, but also our relationships, our views of the world, and our sense of self. The lasting mental health impacts of a collective trauma vary from person to person, depending on their stress at the time, prior trauma history, and whether their relationships are meaningful.[92] It can hinder someone's ability to cope with stress, see meaning in their life, or enjoy simple pleasures. It can also lead to PTSD and anxiety.

Burnout is rife in the social justice space, so Emma has always had strict ways of buffering stress. She meditates and journals and does yoga. She limits social media and avoids email at night. 'You go through life challenges and when the same sorts of things come up, hopefully you deal with it better than you did the first time,' she told me. 'I think what gets easier is that I recognise the signs earlier and I am much better at dealing with it. I can see the things I need to do. I know what works for me.' Given that forecasters are now gently warning that this may not be the only global pandemic we contend with in the years to come, we can all only hope we hold on to these sorts of self-care measures for next time.

Loneliness was already a public health crisis. The pandemic exacerbated it. In 2017, US Surgeon General Vivek Murthy wrote a cover story for the *Harvard Business Review*, declaring an 'epidemic of loneliness': 'We live in the most technologically connected age in the history of civilization,' he wrote. 'Yet rates of loneliness have doubled since the 1980s.'[93] In 2018, Britain appointed its first Minister for Loneliness. Loneliness is associated with a greater risk of depression, anxiety, dementia, and suicide. Studies have also linked loneliness and social isolation to cancer, diabetes and heart disease. It impacts our day-to-day work lives, limiting creativity and reducing our decision-making capabilities. Murthy has also written that loneliness is 'associated with a reduction in lifespan similar to that caused by smoking fifteen cigarettes a day.'

Loneliness is defined as 'a distressing experience that occurs when a person's social relationships are perceived by that person to be less in quantity, and especially quality, than desired. The experience of loneliness is highly subjective; an individual can be alone without feeling lonely and can feel lonely even when with other people.' Before the pandemic, a quarter of Australians were lonely.[94] The Australian Bureau of Statistics' national survey on the household impacts on Covid-19 found that nearly a third of women and 16 per cent of men felt lonely as a result of the pandemic. In the first findings of an ongoing study of more than 2500 Australians, Swinburne University found that one in two Australians feel lonelier since the pandemic began.

In the early months of 2021, Japan appointed Tetsushi Sakamoto as the minister responsible for dealing with isolation and loneliness after a spike in national suicide rates – particularly among women – for the first time in eleven years. According to *Nikkei*, Japan's largest financial newspaper, the number of suicides in Japan in 2020 increased by 3.9 per cent to a total of 20 919 deaths.[95] According to *The Japan Times*, this is three times the number of people who died from Covid-19 in Japan in the same year.[96] A major concern among psychologists is that sustained social isolation will lead to chronic loneliness even after the pandemic has ended. As psychotherapist Yuko Nippoda told the BBC, 'When people experience stress in the outside world, they can detach themselves from that world. Once they experience this detachment, it might be difficult for them to come out into the world and socialise with others.'[97]

Souad Saied is an Australian citizen who moved to Singapore just before the virus officially became a global emergency. She has tried to temper her feelings of loneliness by predicting the end of the pandemic. When there was a glimmer of hope in the news cycle, Souad would book a holiday, only to cancel it weeks later. She would be optimistic some days, hopeless others. She spent the beginning of the pandemic bouncing in and out of denial, which is one of those famous stages of grieving. And that's precisely what Souad – and the rest of us – have been doing. We've all been cycling through the five stages of grief, as outlined by Elisabeth Kübler-Ross and David Kessler in 1986: denial, anger, bargaining, depression and acceptance. Souad told me she felt them all, but she especially threw herself into the denial. Denial helps us pace ourselves in grief and helps us to initially survive the loss. Over time, as you begin to accept the reality of the loss, it fades, and the healing process begins. For Souad, that happened in a single morning.

In July of 2020, the thirty-one-year-old woke up with the same unease she had been living with for months and she decided it was enough. Rather like me, Souad had been half-treating the pandemic as some sort of self-improvement spree, hoping to emerge from it fitter, healthier and better than ever. But she was stressed, anxious and intermittently depressed. That morning, she had a shift in perspective, as denial gave way to a little bit of acceptance. 'I just decided that I was going to get up and assume this is my life from now on. That's it. This is my life now. So how would I live it if this was my life now?' she told me. 'And honestly, the second I did that, I felt radically different. I have definitely had my moments of weakness, but I've never regressed back to the point where I was before I made that decision.'

She couldn't have the big social circle she'd imagined or travel the world like she wanted. But she could perhaps work on the way she ran her life. She swapped her dogged ambition to be productive for a desire to be calm and healthy. She bought a desk from IKEA and set up her home office. She cancelled her HIIT training and replaced it with yoga. She began her workdays at 10 am. The loneliness hasn't entirely gone, but she feels more capable of living with it. 'It definitely becomes easier to manage when you spend more time focusing on how you need to adapt to this situation to make it work for you, rather than trying to change a situation that you simply don't have the power to change.'

Ashna Basu woke up with a headache. It was September 2020, her first year as a junior doctor at a hospital in Sydney. She'd spent the year working in the psychiatric, geriatrics, and neurology departments. She was one of the first doctors in the mental health department to administer a Covid-19 swab test and all the while, like all frontline workers, Ashna was quietly taking the trauma home with her every day. When the pandemic began, her holiday leave was cancelled and after that, she basically didn't stop working. When the lockdown in Sydney ended, Ashna was in her third term and burnout had arrived. She had spent months in the geriatrics department, treating patients particularly vulnerable to Covid-19, and was now in the neurology department treating stroke patients. Ashna felt isolated, alone, and exhausted. People like Ashna are saving lives, protecting the elderly, putting themselves at risk, but who is there to look after them when they slip into bed after an epic shift on the frontline of a global pandemic?

In China, the first country to be confronted by the pandemic, a survey of more than 7000 people measured anxiety, depression and poor sleep in an aim to identify the most high-risk groups. The researchers found that healthcare workers had the highest rate of poor sleep and anxiety symptoms. More than a third of respondents were experiencing anxiety symptoms and a fifth, depressive symptoms.[98] Unsurprisingly, Ashna wasn't the only healthcare worker with a headache. Almost 70 per cent of respondents to a study in China reported physical symptoms such as insomnia, lethargy and headaches – with headaches being the most common.[99] Having adequate PPE has also had mental health implications, with a study out of the UK revealing that healthcare workers who had inadequate equipment were at greater risk of experiencing mental health problems, PTSD, physical health and emotional problems.[100]

From the frontline, Ashna saw right from the beginning how poorly prepared and organised the federal government was in response to the pandemic. She couldn't understand why they hadn't stockpiled PPE and masks. SARS (Severe Acute Respiratory Syndrome) had occurred from 2002 until 2004 – surely the government should have been prepared for another pandemic? 'To me, it's such colonial ignorance to assume that what happened in Asia wouldn't happen here,' she told me. 'Especially with globalisation. That really irritated me.' Ashna was furious with people for not wearing masks, for exercising five times a day so they could see five different friends, for flocking to the beach like it was a festival. 'You had no control over what was happening, but you were the person that was going to have to clean up everyone else's mess.' Eventually, she questioned what the system had done to fail these people. 'It definitely highlighted the importance of government communication. The government eventually had a response, but for a while, it was radio silence. Months into the pandemic, it was still the same really rudimentary surface-level ads,' Ashna told me. 'I think what we've done wrong is just telling people to do things without explaining why. And it was like, well, if the government's not doing that and if the health system's not putting out practical, trustworthy information, other people are jumping in and filling that void. And now Pete Evans is selling a salt lamp.'

For a while, Ashna tried to make up for this failing by posting about Covid-19 on her Instagram stories. Explaining what the virus was, why it was dangerous, why you needed to wash your hands. She had a hugely positive response but then people began direct messaging her with every kind of pandemic question: whether they could have a party or have someone over for dinner or visit their girlfriend who works in a hospital. 'You're exhausted and making decisions for people and just having to be the bad guy all the time,' she told me. 'I know, for a lot of doctors, it's really exhausting being the arbiter of what is and is not acceptable.'

A lot of the doctors Ashna knows have been feeling ostracised because they've been asked not to attend social events or come to family dinners. The hospital told staff to wear civilian clothes outside because nurses were being spat on by members of the public, mirroring a rise in attacks on healthcare workers worldwide.[101] 'On the one hand, everyone's like, "Thank you, frontline worker, you're amazing",' said Ashna. 'On the other hand, people think you're a safety risk because you're more likely to have the infection. And that was a difficult one, because I kind of am.'

When Lexie Dennis was diagnosed with Covid-19, all she felt was a deep sense of guilt. She was General Manager of the Bupa Edithvale aged care home in Melbourne's outer south-east, where they were trying to contain a major coronavirus outbreak. Now she wasn't allowed in the building. On 16 July 2020, during Melbourne's second wave, a staff member had tested positive. PPE was secured, everything was covered in plastic, family members were called, and the Department of Health and Human Services were informed. However, they delayed contact tracing and testing for around five days, the reason for which remains unknown. During that time, management at the aged care home started their own contact tracing system and quickly discovered the infected staff member had been in contact with twenty-seven residents before realising he was sick. By the time official testing began, it was too late.

Over the next two months, forty-four of the seventy residents contracted the virus. Lexie was one of thirty-four staff to be infected. By the time the home was cleared of cases in mid-September, eighteen residents had lost their lives. 'There is still a lot of grief and a lot of trauma,' Lexie told me over the phone. 'Despite doing everything we could, we still lost residents and lots of residents did test positive. Some of the staff felt guilty because they got the virus and some felt guilty because they didn't. And some who made the choice to take some leave during the pandemic because they might have been older themselves or had health issues, now they feel guilty.' Lexie's husband and daughter also contracted the virus, so her own guilt was compounded. She carried an emotional burden for bringing Covid-19 into their home and felt like she had abandoned her staff. She had left them on the frontline while she lay in bed, doing what she could from her laptop. She was the sickest she had ever been and was unable to work for three weeks.

The number of staff who fell ill grew so large that Bupa had to send in management from interstate to help handle the workload. The staff who were still able to work often did double shifts, working eighteen hours a day, seven days a week. The work itself was traumatising and exhausting. There was the general caretaking required of a normal workday, but a second workload caused by the outbreak. Every time a staff member entered a resident's room, they would have to change into a fresh set of PPE, so they were constantly undressing and redressing. Family members needed to be updated all the time. When a resident fell ill and was sent to hospital, there was the possibility you may never see them again. Then there was the additional anxiety that they could pass away alone, unable to have family or friends close by. And there was the grief. 'You just can't put into words the fatigue and how hard everyone worked during that time,' Lexie said.

Once the outbreak was contained, fear lingered in the corridors of the home. 'The first week or so when the doors were open, and we were allowed to come out, a lot of residents didn't. They wanted to stay in their rooms because it had been so long, and they had a routine of having meals come into their rooms and not having to go out. So, it did take a little bit of encouragement for everyone to get back to their old routines.' The collective hesitancy reflected the quiet strength of the residents. Many maintained positive attitudes through the worst. Lexie told me the residents often ended up consoling their own families, who were riddled with worry, and the staff, who were exhausted and anxious. This, she said, is a testament to the adversity they had already faced throughout their long and diverse lives.

Marlene Robbins is a mother to five sons and has lived at Edithvale for the past five years. After the deaths of two husbands, she lived on her own for a few years before growing lonely. She was apprehensive about going into a home but it took her 'all of two hours to know that I'd come to the right place'. There was something about the atmosphere that made her feel at home, she said, and gave her a sense of belonging. The staff accepted her as part of their family. She's always made friends easily and Edithvale was no different.

Aged care facilities were completely devastated by Melbourne's second wave of Covid-19. When I spoke to Marlene, I expected to hear from a woman grappling with isolation, loneliness and grief. It was quite the opposite. When the pandemic began, Marlene was relieved to be at Edithvale.

'The only thing I can say that sums up how I feel about living here is that this is my home,' she said. 'Otherwise, I'd be on my own. My life has changed dramatically since I've been here.' When lockdown began, Marlene couldn't mix with her friends anymore and was confined to her room, but the sense of belonging didn't waver. She could still look out her window. She could still knit and crochet and embroider and colour in. She could still read her books. She read Tom Clancy and Judith Prance and Kathy Reichs.

When the outbreak happened, Marlene had to move out of her room because her neighbour had contracted the virus. One of the hardest parts of those two months was the fact that everyone was so close but there was a level of confidentiality that had to be upheld. The staff weren't allowed to tell Marlene who had contracted the virus, so she worried for her closest friends. She kept knitting and reading and felt grateful to have people close by. 'This is my home. I feel like people care about me,' she said. 'I felt for all the people outside because I'm eighty, and if I go, I go. I'm not going to be here forever. That part didn't worry me. It just worried me how it would affect other people.' During the Edithvale outbreak, Marlene's closest friends survived, but she did lose some friends. 'In places like this, we're all friends really, because you're with them every day,' Marlene told me. 'It does hit you when one of them passes away.'

Lexie hopes there will be reforms in the aged care sector resulting in greater funding so that homes can employ more staff, including psychologists and social workers. Research shows social isolation is particularly detrimental to the elderly, who may have increased risk of anxiety, depression, worsening dementia and early death.[102] Lexie also hopes the wider community will show more care for the elderly population moving forward. She's been deeply offended by the way some people have spoken about the elderly as though they're disposable, or their lives are worth less than younger generations. These haven't been private mutterings either; commentators with radio shows and newspaper columns to fill have made the case for essentially sacrificing the elderly to protect the economy. 'I get quite upset about that, because our residents have lived such interesting lives and have contributed to society so much. To then not value their lives as much as a school child's or someone of working age, that's so offensive,' she told me. 'People just don't understand that when you're living with our residents, they're people and they have really important places in their families. So they are not replaceable, they're not disposable.'

As Edithvale slowly recovers, counselling lines have been set up for the staff to process the trauma confidentially and a memorial committee has been put together. Lexie told me they intend to create a memorial garden as a reminder of what they endured. 'It's definitely something that we don't want to forget.' And neither should the rest of us.

By August 2020, I'd stopped doing yoga, my $83 serum had run out, and I was emotionally depleted. Lockdown was over but my mental health was somehow worse. Then my friend texted to announce that our therapist had gone on maternity leave. 'Just when my mental breakdown is looming,' she wrote. 'I have ninety-nine problems and our therapist is now one.' I understood why essential workers and mothers homeschooling daughters and people living overseas and people who'd lost loved ones felt awful. I couldn't understand why, with my privilege and proximity to the ocean and relative freedoms, I did too.

Later, I read an article called 'Your Surge Capacity Is Depleted – It's Why You Feel Awful' on *Medium*. It instantly went viral and the answer became clear. We were all exhausted by this pandemic, no matter where we lived, who was close by, or how we'd been affected. What we were all experiencing was a depleted surge capacity. Ann Masten, a psychologist and professor of child development at the University of Minnesota, defines 'surge capacity' as a collection of adaptive systems – mental and physical – that humans draw on for short-term survival in acutely stressful situations. Surge capacity is something commonly used by humans in natural disasters, where the devastation may be vast but the event itself occurs relatively quickly. In an immediate emergency, that's useful, but sustaining that through an ongoing pandemic is an entirely different story.

In December 2020, a few weeks before Christmas, I spoke to Ann Masten over Zoom. The professor studies resilience with a particular focus on how children and families adapt when their lives are threatened by adversity. She is interested in integrating resilience theory across disciplines to help address recovery following major disasters and war. She said we have all been reaching surge capacity in some way. 'People were using a lot of their short-term capacity to create an energy and optimism that humans use to cope with challenges and many, many people got burnt out,' she told me. 'I think people are learning how to pace themselves.'

Throughout the pandemic, Masten suffered her own losses – a friend in New York who took their own life at the beginning of lockdown, the challenge of teaching virtually, the disappearance of work travel – but she hoped to remain as useful as possible. She tries to accept every interview request and is sharing what she's learned about resilience with as many people as she can. She knows we need it now more than ever, but she also believes we'll need this knowledge to help us cope in future years. 'This pandemic, I think, is a wake-up call for the future because we're going to have more pandemics,' Masten told me. 'And we're getting close to the tipping point of climate change. That's going to create very profound mass trauma and adversity around the globe.'

The day before we spoke, Masten had noticed the coinciding hope and loss appearing on her television. The death toll displayed in the corner of the screen revealed that America was now losing more citizens each day than they had lost in September 11, but it was accompanied by footage of the first Pfizer vaccines being deployed. The uncertainty and ambiguity we had been living with since the start of the pandemic had been diluted with a good dose of hope. So many of us are still dealing with ambiguous loss, though.

Ambiguous loss is a theory developed by Pauline Boss, a colleague of Masten's who works as a professor emeritus of social sciences at the University of Minnesota, and the author of *Ambiguous Loss: Learning to Live with Unresolved Grief.*[103] Boss defines it as a loss that lacks resolution or is complicated by the challenges of uncertainty. The loss itself feels abstract or unclear, which makes it more difficult to process. There are two different types of ambiguous loss: physical and psychological. A physical loss is when someone is physically missing but psychologically present in people's minds – like a soldier missing at war whose family still holds on to hope that they're alive. A psychological loss is when someone is psychologically missing but physically here – like a dementia patient whose family can still sit beside them.

Pauline Boss believes the pandemic is riddled with ambiguous loss. We are facing an enemy we can't see. It's taken lives, closed businesses and changed the course of our future as a species. On top of the growing death toll and economic turmoil, there's the loss of things about life that felt essential to the way we lived. The loss of our regular routines, being able to hug a loved one, the freedom to do whatever we want, to travel, seeing family and friends, even going to a game of cricket or standing at a sweaty gig. For many people, there's also a loss of trust in our government and a loss of faith in one another. 'These losses are not the ones we have sympathy cards or rituals to deal with, and grief for these losses often gets stuck because there are no supports for it … What we need to do now is name these losses. You can't cope with something until you have a name for it.'

Even the finish line for the pandemic remains ambiguous, along with what is on the other side. 'I know people who are experiencing all kinds of loss, and not just loss by death, but loss of hopes and dreams and opportunities,' Ann Masten told me. 'There's a lot of postponing of life transitions that have the quality of ambiguous loss, because you don't know what might have been.' There's the young woman who spends her first year of university without an on-campus experience. The graduate who can't find a job. The restaurant owner who loses her entire business. The bride who cancels her wedding. 'A dream lost is different from a dream postponed,' Masten told me. 'It's very difficult, and I think people cope in many different ways. Sometimes they find a different dream. Sometimes people can find a different path. One of the great coping strategies people have is their flexibility, and we are all having to alter our lives, at least in the short-term; and in many cases, I think, for longer than we were expecting.'

For Souad Saied, this ambiguous loss is the joy of a particular lifestyle. For Emma Fulu, it's the feeling of expansion she gets from travelling for work. For Ashna Basu, this loss is, perhaps, faith in government leaders. For Lexie Dennis and Marlene Robbins, it's the loss of eighteen people they spent the majority of their days with. And for Anna Liptak, who continues to feel the long-term effects of Covid-19, this loss is her good health.

After Anna was cleared of the coronavirus and reunited with her husband, life was meant to return to normal, but it didn't. She had regular headaches and was constantly tired. She usually ran four or five times a week, but now, if she ran too fast, too far, or too often, she would end up back in bed. 'When I no longer had Covid-19, that was it: "You no longer have Covid-19." There was no one to follow up about my symptoms, no one telling me where to go or what to do or go and check my heart or my lungs or anything like that,' Anna told me. 'You have to circumnavigate it yourself.'

Many of us know someone who has had ongoing health problems following Covid-19. What is perhaps most surprising is these people aren't just the elderly or the chronically ill. They are young and healthy people like Anna. More than 116 million people have contracted the coronavirus, and research has shown that about a third of them will have long-lasting symptoms that continue past the initial two weeks. These people are often called 'long-haulers' and the ongoing disease is called post-acute Covid-19 syndrome, or 'long-Covid'. Research from the Centers for Disease Control and Prevention states that these lingering symptoms can include fatigue, confusion, loss of taste or smell, headaches, body aches, diarrhoea, nausea, chest or abdominal pain, cough, congestion or shortness of breath.[104] A phone survey revealed that two to three weeks after testing positive to the coronavirus, 35 per cent of people had not returned to their usual state of health. And while you might assume that was mostly the elderly and immunocompromised, the survey revealed that one in five people aged between eighteen and thirty-four years with no chronic medical conditions had not returned to their regular state of health.

According to The World Health Organization, little is known about the clinical course of Covid-19 following milder illness. However, it claims the virus may increase long-term health problems.[105] These problems can include damage to the heart muscle,[106] heart failure, damage to lung tissue, restrictive lung failure, loss of smell, cognitive impairment, pain in joints and muscles, and fatigue. It can also affect consequences of thrombo-embolic events such as pulmonary embolism, heart attack and stroke. Looking back through history also suggests that for many, the recovery from the coronavirus will be a long and enduring road. A study looking at the long-term impact of SARS in 2003 showed there was a significant and persistent impairment of exercise capacity and health status in survivors of SARS over the following two years.[107] Another study revealed that 40 per cent of SARS survivors experienced chronic fatigue symptoms for another three-and-a-half years.[108]

The future impact of Covid-19 does not just include the physical. The virus can affect our mental health, often triggering anxiety, depression, sleep disturbance, and post-traumatic stress disorder. There are stories of people experiencing psychosis. In March 2020, a study of 714 clinically stable Covid-19 patients in Wuhan found that 96.2 per cent had significant PTSD symptoms.[109] And, looking back, an analysis of twenty-eight studies looking into the long-term clinical outcomes of SARS and MERS (Middle East Respiratory Syndrome) survivors showed that 39 per cent of adults who were in ICU had experienced PTSD beyond six months of discharge. Thirty-three per cent experienced depression and another 30 per cent, anxiety.[110] Research by Italian academics concludes that we should expect similar outcomes in survivors of Covid-19 in the future.[111]

In the United States, non-profits and institutes have been set up to treat people experiencing 'long-Covid'. Anna thinks we need those support systems in Australia too. 'There are thousands of people in Australia that have been affected who are scrambling on Facebook to find answers,' she said. Anna found herself turning to the Facebook page of Survivor Corps,[112] a not-for-profit dedicated to educating Covid-19 survivors. The page has 154 700 followers who share their experiences and photos of family members they have lost. Most often they compare lingering side effects. Some are battling insomnia, losing their hair, getting strange pains on the side of their chest, and some are constantly hungry despite being unable to smell or taste anything.

The Facebook page has helped Anna stay informed and feel less alone in her suffering. Anna is still experiencing chronic fatigue, headaches, tightness in her chest, and inflammation of her respiratory system. When we spoke on the phone, her voice was different from the first time we spoke. In between our two phone calls, she'd had surgery on her nose to help her breathe more easily. Her heart and lungs have been scarred and the doctors are unable to tell whether this was caused by the virus, but they suspect it is. The scarring may continue to grow but, like everything else, Anna sits with the uncertainty. 'I have my up days where I feel completely great, and then I go down so hard. And it's not depression, it's just fatigue and an overwhelming sense of crushing in my lungs,' she said.

'You can hear it in my breath even when I talk to you that there's something not right. And there are no answers. Will it get worse? We don't know.'

Anna has experienced anxiety because there's so much unknown about her physical health, a loss of confidence in her body, and financial stress due to the decimation of her second business, Adventure Time Travel, which organises group fitness holidays to events such as the New York Marathon. As Anna focuses on rebuilding her business and her sense of self, managing her mental health alongside living with the enduring physical effects of the virus, she gets solidarity from other people still living with illness. 'I know people who have lost incomes, I know people who have lost family members. So, you know, I think everyone's been dealt a different card and it's affected everyone so differently,' she told me. 'That's what's weird about it, is that everyone is affected, whether you've had it or not. Yesterday, I was reading about a lady who had fourteen members of her family have it, and twelve have died. I can't even imagine that. It's a different loss for everybody in different ways. Mine may be physical, mental and financial at the moment. It's a dark space, but I can still see light for myself. I'm sure there are some people who have lost their husbands and children and I'm not sure they can see the light.'

Over the past 12 000 years, pandemics have killed an estimated 300–500 million people.[113] When we try to predict the future impacts of a pandemics, it helps to look back. History has shown us that the mental health impact of disasters like the Covid-19 pandemic often outlasts the physical impact. Following the SARS outbreak in 2003, research revealed a 30 per cent increase in suicides in people over the age of sixty-five.[114] Five years after Hurricane Katrina devastated New Orleans in 2005, mental health problems – such as post-traumatic stress disorder and psychological distress – persisted in people who had lost their homes.[115] Mothers who had lower incomes or poorer mental health before the hurricane also had more pronounced mental health problems. But perhaps the most notable piece of research comes from a twenty-five-year review of the impact of the Chernobyl accident in Ukraine. More than 4000 people died and the nation's economy was decimated, but researchers concluded that the toll it took on people's mental health was the most significant consequence. Two decades later, first responders still had elevated rates of PTSD and depression.[116]

Psychologists and public health officials are becoming increasingly concerned about the long-lasting mental health problems caused by the pandemic. A meta-analysis of the psychological toll outbreaks have on healthcare workers found that psychological distress can last for up to three years following an outbreak like the coronavirus. Author of *The*

Psychology of Pandemics Steven Taylor has said that 'for an unfortunate minority of people, perhaps 10 to 15 per cent, life will not return to normal.'[117] In 2020, an analysis released in May by the Well Being Trust and the Robert Graham Center for Policy Studies in Family Medicine and Primary Care projected a rise in 'deaths of despair' in the United States due to sustained social isolation and the coinciding financial crises. They have projected that as many as 75 000 more people will die from suicide and alcohol or drug misuse.[118]

Professor Ian Hickie, Co-Director of Health and Policy at The University of Sydney's Brain and Mind Centre, says we will be feeling the mental health fallout from the pandemic across Australia for at least the next five years. For younger people, it's expected to last for the next ten. During the pandemic there have been significant increases in anxiety, depression, sleep disturbance, self-harm and suicidal ideation. Up to 50 per cent of the population were talking about anxiety and depression at the height of lockdown, especially women and young people. Hickie and his colleagues are now tracking reports of a 20 per cent increase in self-harm and suicidal behaviour in young people. Again, this trend is increasing at higher rates in women more than men. 'The effects on psychological welfare and on really serious complications like suicidal ideation and suicide attempts, as predicted, are all going in the wrong direction,' he told me. 'The only thing that hasn't gone up, which may go up, is actual deaths by suicide, which tends to be a phenomenon of men between twenty-five and fifty. I think what we're seeing is the positive effects of employment and other supports, such as JobKeeper, being extended throughout the whole of last year.' To date, government support has focused on lifting the business sector and classically male-dominated industries such as construction and mining, while education funding has gone towards apprenticeships and trades.

The two biggest threats to people's overall mental health, according to Hickie, is the ongoing impact on employment, education and financial security, and the ongoing impact on social networks, families and other social structures. When families were forced to stay in their homes, women were dangerously affected by the pressures of dealing with domestic and professional responsibilities. Numerous studies have linked ongoing unemployment or loss of income to depression, stress, or suicidal thoughts.[119] A lot of those job losses are happening to workers in the hospitality, tourism and caring industries such as teaching, nursing, aged care, and childcare. Those who are most affected during these downturns, said Hickie, are people already in less secure, less skilled employment, and those who have fewer assets and resources. 'So who has got fewer assets in the first place? Who has less secure work? Who has less security? And who has been least supported by government initiatives? It's women and young people, so if you're young and female, you're doubly disadvantaged,' he said. 'Recessions kill the margin, right? That's particularly true in rural and regional Australia, it's true outside the cities and any areas that were already affected by the drought, the bushfires, unemployment opportunities, and they were most dependent on tourism and hospitality. So in Australia, from southeast Queensland, right down the coast to part of New South Wales, right into Victoria, these areas that are really where all of that casual work that has got high female participation is really dependent on the industries that have been affected. So there's also differentials by place as well.'

Australians have already been affected by the Black Summer bushfires, and the pandemic has only compounded these effects. The need for funding in the mental healthcare sector is urgent. In a report titled 'Rethinking Mental Health in Australia', Professor Hickie and his colleagues outline the fundamental principles they believe should underpin mental healthcare reform in Australia. While our health system is frequently heralded one of the best in the world, they wrote, this does not apply to mental health 'where Australia is far from world-class'. As the pandemic has increased the community's risk of anxiety, depression, financial distress, social isolation, unemployment and educational dislocation, we desperately need a renewed investment in our psychological wellbeing. 'Mental health was typically characterised as in crisis before Covid-19,' they said. 'There is widespread recognition that

Australia's mental health system is palpably inadequate for the challenges ahead.'[120]

While the National Mental Health Commission is currently working on a 'Vision 2030' for mental health, the authors warned that the government has historically invested in '20th century models of mental health care' which do not meet the current national needs, or acknowledge the specific challenges caused by Covid-19. 'The pandemic has provided a definitive message. Business as usual approaches that prioritise traditional, very centralised, top-down mental health planning mechanisms just will not work and are not good strategies. Repurposing the past is not an option. Consequently, there is an urgent need to design a contemporary, responsive and effective mental health system, that learns from the past but is fit for Australia in the 21st century.'

For too long, we've failed to recognise how much the mental health of Australian citizens impacts our economic performance as a nation. Mental ill-health and suicide cost the Australian economy anywhere from $43 to $51 billion each year, according to the 2019 draft report of the Productivity Commission. On top of this, there is the estimated $130 billion cost associated with deteriorating health and reduced life expectancy of those living with mental ill-health. As the 'Rethinking Mental Health in Australia' report states, 'The case for investing in population mental health and wellbeing is not only morally and socially compelling, it is economically fundamental.' Will the deadly impacts of a global pandemic be enough to convince the government to see that? We can only hope.

One of the exciting changes we've seen in health care recently is the expansion of telehealth. During the pandemic, the government made it available to more people. People are more willing to use it, more often, because they can seek care without having to leave their home, or their children, or their workplace. They can save travel time and transport costs. That's all great, but Hickie thinks it could become even better if we take cues from this pandemic to make lasting improvements to our health sector. 'What is really required is digital health. Not just doing the same as what you would do in your office, over Zoom or FaceTime, but actually doing things differently. Much more frequent, shorter, much more empowering forms of care, much more triaging of care, much better assisting people,' he said. 'In the modelling we have done, digital care could have a big effect. The whole thing is: right care, first time.'

Hickie's personal belief is that the market for digital health is so strong, the private sector is beginning to capitalise on it worldwide and will continue to do so in the years (and pandemics) to come. 'You're going to see private sector stuff happen very quickly. Worldwide, the demand is huge. If you look at what we are doing in most of our health systems, you'd think we're somewhere about 1998.'

Here's hoping the horrific consequences of a deadly global pandemic will be enough to inspire our leaders to drag our healthcare system into this century.

This virus has caused damage in ways we haven't even thought of yet. Seriously ill people have been exposed to further risk without ever drawing a shallow, Covid-shortened breath. Stay-at-home orders have pushed back elective surgeries and rocked community confidence in the health system, which has caused further complications and delays. When lockdown began in Australia in March 2020, non-elective surgeries were put on hold. Surgeries were triaged by urgency and at this time, surgeries that needed to be performed within 30 days – such as removing a melanoma – were allowed, but all other surgeries had to wait. In April, restrictions were loosened to allow surgeries that needed to be performed within 90 days to go ahead. Those were surgeries like hernia repair or conducting a laparoscopy on someone with pelvic pain to diagnose endometriosis. Surgeries that needed to occur within one year, such as knee and hip replacements or cataract surgery or a follow-up colonoscopy, have been the most affected by delays.

Chair of the Royal Australasian College of Surgeons NSW state committee Payal Mukherjee, who is also an ear, nose and throat surgeon, told me that these elective surgeries are not life-threatening, but they can really affect a person's quality of life. In Victoria, where elective surgeries were delayed for even longer due to the second wave, the impact is massive. As the world shut down and went virtual all at once, some of Mukherjee's deaf and elderly patients struggled to communicate through the telephone and Zoom. 'There are a lot of elderly patients who were really isolated and unable to communicate with anybody,' she said. 'Lockdown was a long time for them, and we know that these conditions have a real impact on other neurocognitive decline. If you're locked up and not able to communicate, the brain atrophies much quicker. So, across the board, from children to adults and elderly, you cause harm by a lack of access to health care.'

Organ donation and transplants have also been widely affected in countries with high rates of Covid-19, including the United States, Spain, the United Kingdom and France. These countries have all reported more than a 50 per cent reduction in transplant activity. While Australia has fared better in this respect, the impact on organ donation and transplantation has still been significant. When the pandemic began, a taskforce of organ donation and transplantation experts was set up in Australia and New Zealand. They recommended suspending all adult kidney transplants while urgent heart, lung, liver and paediatric transplantations continued on a case-by-case basis. Experts feared patients may contract the coronavirus in hospitals after their operation, and that the growing number of Covid-19 cases would limit capacity in ICU beds, which could compromise transplant patients. By mid-April 2020, when cases had slowed around the country, transplantations were allowed to recommence. However, during the second wave in Victoria, donations and transplants continued but were heavily affected by logistical barriers and border closures. Research published in October 2020 shows that in Australia kidney transplantation activity was down 27 per cent compared to 2019. Liver transplants were down 8 per cent, while heart and pancreas transplants were up 26 per cent and 32 per cent respectively.[121] Globally, the pandemic is having the same negative impact on donations and transplants.

The pandemic also quashed community confidence in the healthcare system. During lockdown people were scared, so they avoided hospitals and GP practices. Dr Neela Janakiramanan, a plastic and reconstructive surgeon and hand and wrist surgeon, believes some people understood that seeking health care was an appropriate reason to leave the house, but others didn't. She says there was an issue with how information was communicated. 'There were lots of people who, even though they knew they could leave the house to seek medical care, didn't want to risk getting pulled over by the police in case they were unable to explain where they were going, and why they were doing it. That fear of policing also meant that people didn't seek medical care when they should,' she said. For example, a patient with chest pain who would normally have had an angiogram, start on blood pressure lowering medications and maybe a blood thinner instead sits at home ignoring that chest pain for six months and then comes in actually having a heart attack. 'Management is more complicated. They then need to go to rehab, they then have permanent muscle damage to the heart. And then you start wondering, did they have that heart attack because they have this underlying predisposition or because of the stress that was caused by the fact that people have lost their jobs, there's housing insecurity, there's domestic violence, there's women who have been left behind in the economic market? We know all of these things have an impact on health. So there's that long-term effect that we're going to be dealing with as well.'

As hospitals reached capacity and the subsequent fear around visiting an emergency department grew, many GPs and specialists performed procedures they wouldn't normally perform. For example, patients would have a couple of stitches at their GP rather than presenting to an emergency department. 'We did lots of things that we would not normally do in a developed country in order to provide health care, lots of temporising measures,' Dr Janakiramanan said. 'And so there was a shifting of care from hospitals to the community, with the potential that some of the care that was received was not entirely optimal. And some of those results we won't see for a long time because you can't possibly know what happened.'

The lack of community confidence during the pandemic has also reduced important health screenings, which is a huge issue. In March 2021, Cancer Council's Victorian branch published concerning figures in the *Medical Journal of Australia* showing that there had been a 10 per cent reduction in cancer screening pathology tests between April and October in 2020.[122] That could mean up to 2530 missed cancer diagnoses in Victoria. The Cancer Council has warned that could potentially cause a 'cancer spike' later on. During the first six months of the pandemic, there was also a 30 per cent drop in cancer diagnostic procedures and an 18 per cent drop in treatments. Dr Mukherjee told me about a patient she'd seen after lockdown who had metastatic cancer which had spread everywhere by the time she saw him. If she had seen him six weeks earlier, it would have been an entirely different story.

The alarming flow-on effects of delayed surgeries and care are even felt in states like Western Australia, where there have been low Covid-19 numbers, she said. Dr Janakiramanan told me about a man in Perth whose colonoscopy was postponed by lockdown, and again after lockdown because of the backlog of urgent surgeries. By the time he had his colonoscopy, the doctors found bowel cancer which had become terminal. Most of her colleagues in plastic surgery have seen more advanced skin cancers and have consequently sent more patients off for radiotherapy options because they are treating cancers that are more advanced by the time they remove them. 'So additional treatment has been required, and that creates extra work within the health system,' she said. 'As a direct impact of the pandemic and people not presenting for care, this has created a burden of disease.' We may never know how vast that burden of disease is. What we do know is that the pressure on the health system will continue to be felt into the future.

'You have a scenario where we feel like we're providing universal health care, but the reality is that there are a large number of health conditions for which we actually are not providing particularly good care or any care at all,' Dr Janakiramanan said. If she wanted to refer someone with rheumatoid arthritis to see a public rheumatologist, they might wait two or three years. 'The amount of pain and disability caused by that wait, sometimes can't be recovered. So there's permanent damage done and the pandemic has actually worsened all of that. So now we have a scenario where hospitals are flooded by the backlog of work. And it's also flooded with these mental health issues, and the issues that have arisen because timely management hasn't taken place during the pandemic.'

Again, there are huge opportunities for change and innovation here, if only we grasp them. Crisis has always been the mother of invention. Dr Stephen Duckett, Health Program Director at The Grattan Institute, believes our experience with Covid-19 has enabled the Australian health system to change extremely rapidly. 'There was a pivot to telehealth that might have otherwise taken years to achieve, and this will have a number of implications,' he told me. Telehealth can be used for consultations but also monitoring of conditions, like helping patients manage chronic illness more easily and in the comfort of their own homes, or getting more rural patients involved in clinical trials so that they have access to the same new therapies as people living in cities. If we're smart about it, we could totally transform the way we treat illness, injury and medical care.

Dr Duckett said there has been an enormous amount of innovation across the healthcare sector already – a hopeful, galvanising by-product of an otherwise horrifying global crisis. 'The risks of not innovating were higher than the risks of innovating,' he told me. 'So it unleashed an enormous amount of energy in hospital and health service staff to actually do and try new things.' We all saw how quickly multiple vaccines have been developed when scientists are given urgent, adequate funding (sometimes by government officials, sometimes by Dolly Parton). For Dr Mukherjee, the most exciting thing was how quickly research was done. 'The type of research that we've had across the board has been unheard of and unseen in a century,' she said. The real-time exchange of data around the world has seen medical publications and journals that would usually take six months, turned around and published fantastically quickly.

'I think what we've seen through this crisis is a massive opportunity to improve our systems,' Dr Mukherjee said. 'And that's what I'm hoping is going to be the next focus. There's still a lot of work to do.' While Dr Janakiramanan hopes the pressure of the pandemic will spur genuine health system reform, Dr Duckett hopes the healthcare sector will continue to build on the momentum they've had. 'It's easy to slip back into the old ways. The hope, of course, is that we don't. I've got hope that we will be creating a more innovative health system, building on the energy and the innovation that took place during Covid.'

One of the loveliest examples of Covid-inspired positive change came from our First Nations communities. Aboriginal Community Controlled Health Organisations have shown how effective health communication can play a leading role in reducing the devastation of a pandemic. These bodies are supported by state peak bodies but are importantly primary healthcare services run *by* Aboriginal people *for* Aboriginal people. When news of Covid-19 began, chief executive officers responded quickly, lobbying governments to lock down remote communities across Australia. They worked hard and fast to distribute targeted and culturally appropriate social media campaigns explaining what the coronavirus was and what people should do to protect themselves. First Nations communities were badly affected by the 2009 H1N1 influenza epidemic, so they understood the cost of not responding quickly. Aboriginal and Torres Strait Islander people also have higher morbidity and are always expected to be disproportionately impacted by something like the Covid-19 pandemic. In 2020, though, the outcome was reversed. There were only sixty First Nations cases nationwide, which make up only 0.7 per cent of cases in Australia. The First Nations population makes up 3 per cent of the nation. If their rates of transmission were the same as non-Indigenous people, we should have seen 215 cases. And then, when you consider their higher rates of sickness and chronic illness, it should have been even higher than that.

First Nations academic Summer Finlay believes this rapid, targeted response directly accounts for the incredibly low number of cases we've seen across First Nations communities. The social media campaigns began in February 2020, one month before the coronavirus was officially declared a pandemic. We all saw global leaders who took much, much longer than that to treat the pandemic as the global health crisis it was. 'The understanding of the ACCHOs of their communities has allowed them to tailor their communications in a way that external bodies such as governments or other NGOs just can't,' Finlay told me over the phone in December. 'They were able to tailor the social media campaigns and broader communications so they reflected the communities within which they are actually meant to target. So culturally, not just in terms of translating it to first language, but to the vernacular of that community. And because they were coming from a trusted source – the local health service that the actual community used – there was a sense of trust there that you wouldn't always get from, say, a government body.' If we're looking for examples of effective communication and innovation from which to learn, this is a very good place to start.

The urge to find control was quiet, persistent, and felt by almost everyone. We all experimented with new ways to distract and survive and self-soothe. Some of us found comfort in gluten-free banana bread. Others found it in card games or fitness challenges. We all found a small part of our worlds to control in an out-of-control situation. Agency is something we turn to in moments of uncertainty and claiming it for ourselves has proven to help us cope better. The urge was to grab back some control, yes, but it was also something more: a desire to optimise our lockdown experience and perhaps even capitalise on it. The mythology of personal productivity has been fed to us through an intravenous drip for the last two decades. Now it was so firmly embedded in our core, it became an automatic response in a situation like this one. The wellness industry, perhaps predictably, relished the opportunity to give us more things to buy, try and consume in order to become better versions of ourselves.

When stay-at-home orders were enacted around the world, the gyms closed but the wider wellness entrepreneurs and influencers preened for their moment in the sun. We had never had more time for face masks and gratitude journals, so the self-help gurus posted feverishly and wellness companies sold with more force. The products wouldn't just make us better – they would assist us in becoming better prepared to handle Covid-19. Apparently all I required to make it out of this pandemic were some positive affirmations and a $93 elixir that would 'boost my immune system'. As the ingestibles were sold and the affirmations posted, the live streams also began. Live-streamed yoga and live-streamed Pilates and live-streamed HIIT classes and live-streamed dance classes. I danced with Ryan Heffington in LA and with a teacher from Moves Pure Joy in New York. We were joyous and sweaty and slightly deranged. For a moment there, were we actually having fun? It felt innocent and novel and freeing – but the urge to control remained. Soon we were back, becoming better again. Boutique fitness trainers flogged their personal brands on the internet and we all bought in with our post-pandemic body in mind.

The wellness industry has seen some unprecedented changes and, fortunately, the future of wellness is looking more accessible and inclusive. In January, the global wellness booking platform Mindbody released its 2021 Mindbody Wellness Index after surveying almost 20 000 Americans on their wellness habits. Fifty-two per cent of those surveyed were women and the participants were aged between eighteen and sixty-five. The research revealed the emergence of a hybrid model across the fitness industry. More than half of exercisers have decided to split their sweat time between virtual workouts at home and in-person sessions at a studio or gym. Before the pandemic, only 7 per cent of Mindbody users were live streaming workouts on a weekly basis. By late 2020, that number had increased to 85 per cent.

When lockdown began, I cancelled my $65-a-week membership to a boutique fitness studio and signed up to a virtual membership with the yoga studio Sky Ting for $35 a month. Most people I knew did the same, and the majority of us claimed we would never be able to justify the expense of an in-studio membership again. Now, though, I see friends trickling back into studios. The adoption of virtual workouts and rise of the hybrid fitness routine has led to three positive shifts in the industry. The recalibration has democratised fitness, increased the accessibility of 'snackable' workouts, and created a safe space for those too intimidated to attend a studio. While in-studio classes are now smaller and increasingly more expensive, virtual classes are far less expensive and far more accessible. Bite-sized workouts are on the rise, with 39 per cent of Americans surveyed claiming their workouts now last for thirty minutes or less. These kinds of workouts offer even more to the timid gym-goer. According to the research, gym intimidation, or 'gymtimidation', is real, with 12 per cent of participants claiming they are too intimidated to attend a studio or gym. Virtual classes eliminate one of the biggest turn-offs.

After my yoga routine faltered, I cancelled my membership and moved to virtual Pilates. If I had wanted to attend classes in a studio with the likes of Pip Edwards and Elle Ferguson it would cost me $90 a week. The at-home membership I found costs me $20 a month. At some point each day, I roll out my mat and do a twenty-minute workout with a trainer I would never be able to afford before the pandemic arrived. I'm also able to work out in the time it would take me to drive to the studio. The rise of the hybrid fitness model is making fitness less expensive, more accessible, and more inclusive.

It's not just how we exercise that's changing, though. It's *why* we exercise.

We've seen a rise in people exercising for their minds as much as their bodies. Thirty-one per cent of people in the 2021 Mindbody Wellness Index said they were working out because they wanted to feel better mentally. Exercise has predominantly been used as a way to transform our bodies, but when lockdowns occurred, it became one of the only avenues to access the outside world or see a friend. It soon became a tool to help us mentally survive government-mandated time inside. In my own suburb, Bondi, everyone suddenly became a runner to keep themselves sane. I have also seen this shift occur in my own routine. I may do Pilates for twenty minutes each day, which maintains my physical health, but that gives me enough time to walk most mornings and evenings. I walk for my mind more than my body, because I always return home with a sense of mental clarity.

Holly Friend, a trend forecaster at The Future Laboratory, believes the wellness industry is slowly losing the 'be your best self' narrative. 'A lot of wellness brands are promoting fitness and exercise to be "in the moment" because we've forgotten how to centre ourselves and we're always thinking about the future, always thinking about the past,' she told me. 'That shift from physical to mental health, even within physical fitness, is definitely where this is going.' It seems like the future of wellness may be in using it as an activity to sustain ourselves instead of optimise ourselves.

In the brief period of time when I lived in the eastern suburbs of Sydney above a national park, and that long stretch of white sand reflected the possibility of fresh starts, I could see what those fresh starts entailed. It was clear to me that I wanted to embrace a slower, simpler way of living. What remained unclear was whether anyone else felt the same. When I spoke to Holly Friend over the phone in October, during her London morning and my Sydney evening, it was obvious it wasn't just me. A year before our phone call, Friend had begun feeling burnt out by the state of relentless productivity we were being asked to maintain. So as the pandemic took hold, she co-authored a macro-trend report called 'The Pleasure Revolution', published by The Future Laboratory. The report states that every second of our free time has been colonised by the cult of busyness – and we're getting increasingly disillusioned by that as time (and pandemics) go by. The self-actualising activities we have bought into – from the ritual of workism to the wellness industry – are not actually fostering fulfilment but hindering it. We spend our leisure time refining ourselves physically or intellectually, and if we're not doing this, we're feeling guilty about not doing so. 'People still think the narrative is self-improvement: this optimised self,' Friend told me. 'Obviously, the people who are a bit more ahead of the curve will see the backlash against that too, which is where I was coming from. It just felt like we were reaching a point in time where we couldn't really do this anymore.'

As the burnt out and exhausted begin to question the way we are living, we're reassessing what makes a good life. What this life looks like will vary for each one of us, but it is a life where people will begin to embrace inactivity and spontaneous living as much as they once embraced going to the gym before sunrise. In fact, inactivity and rest will become the new signs of success and opting out will become the new opting in, according to Friend. She believes we have already started to see this particular shift. One of the best metaphors for this change, she said, is the rise of loungewear as the new status symbol. We now wear loungewear to display our lifestyle in the same way we once wore activewear. The reason for this shift, of course, is because the message has changed. We once wore activewear to signify our productivity and activity; we now wear loungewear to perform our homebody status. We only have to look to Instagram to see this cultural shift has already occurred. 'The cool "It girl", even before the pandemic, isn't someone who goes out anymore and shows that she's at a party,' Friend told me. 'She's someone who is in her room, looking cute in her loungewear. Maybe she's just ordered a box of natural wine from a subscription service and she's doing her own baking.'

It's easy to see this trend as just another form of self-care that will be capitalised on – and perhaps it will be. However, the crucial part of this trend, Friend said, is the activism element: enjoyment is used as a form of resistance against capitalism. The philosopher, Sandy Grant, is quoted frequently in the trend report. 'In a time when self-improvement practices are big business, enjoyment is a practice of resistance to current forms of unfreedom,' she says.[123]

The trend is currently being led by activists like Grant and, surprisingly or unsurprisingly, Generation Z. 'They want to slow down. They don't want to go out as much. They see the pleasure in the simple things in life,' Friend told me. 'It's more surprising coming from Gen Z because you expect this to be something that people feel as they get older.'

The recalibration towards this slower way of living was predicted to emerge as the 'new normal' by 2030. When I spoke to Friend, she believed the pandemic has sped up its progress and we could be living in this world by 2027. The pandemic has forced us into a period of reflection. Many of us will – if we haven't already – readjust, recalibrate, and perhaps re-emerge with a new pace and different notions of success. Meanwhile, the early adopters of this trend are choosing enjoyment and inactivity to work against the current system, rather than with it, and to possibly create opportunities outside of it.

In her book, *How to Do Nothing: Resisting the Attention Economy*, Jenny Odell argues that we should question the very nature of capitalist productivity, which has left us constantly running, unable to hold on to a clear thought and incapable of seeing each other for who we really are. As social media streamlines our identities into neat personal brands and the mythology of productivity has left us relentlessly implementing more habits to optimise our time, Odell argues that we should readjust our approach to life in general. Life is '*more than an instrument* and therefore something that cannot be optimized,' she writes. 'Solitude, observation, and simple conviviality should be recognised not only as ends in and of themselves, but inalienable rights belonging to anyone lucky enough to be alive.'[124]

The most fulfilled moments of Odell's life have occurred in small, ordinary moments where she was completely aware of her aliveness. 'In those moments, the idea of success as a teleological goal would have made no sense; the moments were ends in themselves, not steps on a ladder.' The book is essentially about how to 'hold open that place in the sun' and motivated by a simple refusal that 'the present time and place, and the people who are here with us, are somehow not enough'. This book came out one year before the pandemic, but when I read it during Melbourne's second lockdown, it felt more like a post-pandemic bible. The lessons Odell teaches us fit neatly into the rearranged priorities so many people are looking forward to on the other side of this global health crisis.

At the start of the pandemic, I felt guilty for doing nothing while people were suffering, even though that was precisely what I needed to do in order to keep strangers and loved ones safe. The problem was not that my desire for a slower, simpler way of living was cast against a backdrop of mass human suffering so much as that my desire for a slower, simpler way of living was intertwined with notions of capitalist productivity. I didn't just want to be toned, clear-headed and calm to live life more fully and be present for the people around me. I wanted to be toned, clear-headed and calm to be *more productive*. This is the paradox, one year later, that I am still working to untangle. The knot has loosened, but it is still there. The solution to this problem isn't found in the accumulation of better habits to optimise my time, but in questioning how I approach life in general.

I began 2021 with no big plans or grand resolutions. There was no desire to develop a significant yoga habit or own an inbox that frequently returned to zero. I entered this year with a single, quiet commitment to readjust how I approach my life. To slow down. To tread a little lighter. To take my constant striving and mould it into an urge that instead pursues those moments of joy and lightness. Those moments where a single second stretches into infinity.

I didn't have a clear plan for how I would do it but as the year has gone on, I have found those moments, again and again, on my daily walks. I walk at the beginning of my day and, again, at the end of it. These walks don't deliver a toned body and there's nothing particularly monumental about them. They are just little pockets of time I have carved out where I listen to music and marvel at the way the light hits the leaves just so. I feel alive and *here* and that feeling sustains me. As a result, I tread through my good days lighter and manage my bad days better.

Bill Murray once said that the more relaxed we are, the better we are at everything. The better we are with our loved ones. The better we are with our enemies. The better we are at our jobs. The better we are with ourselves. He also once said that we have to be available for life. 'We're in this life, and if you're not available, the sort of ordinary time goes past and you didn't live it,' he said. 'But if you're available, life gets huge.'

For the last few years, I have been making plans and executing them but I'm not sure I was really available for life. I was too busy running from one task to the next, from one plan to another, looking so adamantly forward that I forgot to look around. I feel like I'm not alone here. If I was, no one else would be trying to live slower or simpler.

When lockdown ended, it didn't take long before I missed it. I kept that quiet thought to myself because it felt ignorant and stupid but as time has passed and as cities and borders have opened up, I have noticed more people missing the silver linings of that time. I have witnessed friends being pulled back into overly social, busy schedules and putting the handbrake on again. More and more of us, it seems, are having to work harder to hold on to the way of living we saw so clearly when the world had stopped.

If the past eighteen months have taught us anything, it's that there's no point living too far in the future. We make plans and they're cancelled. We book flights and they're refunded. And perhaps our plans being thrown off course, again and again and again and again, is actually teaching us an important lesson. To stop looking forward and instead be here, now. On our walk or with our friends or at our coffee shop or with our kids or lying in bed with our partner. When we pay attention to those moments, life really does get huge.

Odell argues that we don't need to cancel our gym memberships, delete our social media accounts and join a cult in order to live fully. This new way of living we're trying to grasp doesn't mean we can't work important jobs or work out or have traditional success. We can still participate but in a different way. By being online and switching off, by being productive during our workdays, but turning off the laptop at night. In short, she encourages us to disengage, enough. 'Standing apart represents the moment in which the desperate desire to leave (forever!) matures into a commitment to live in permanent refusal,' Odell writes. 'This kind of resistance still manifests as participating but participating in the wrong way: a way that undermines the authority of the hegemonic game and creates possibilities outside of it.' When we stop running and look around, we render new realities for ourselves. When the notifications slow down and the schedules open up, we can pay more attention to the faces directly in front of us and the places in which we live. In this sense, Odell hopes that her book contributes something to activism by providing a 'rest stop for those on their way to fight the good fight'.

Post-traumatic growth is a term used to describe the positive psychological change that can occur in an individual or collective as a result of experiencing adversity. When I think about the future, I keep coming back to this term and something else Pauline Boss told the *Mind of State* podcast in relation to ambiguous loss. 'This is both terrible *and* we may grow from it,' she said. 'This is both a terrible time in our history *and* we may get stronger for it.'[125] During this stretch of time, our collective mental and physical health has taken a hit *and* we are seeing really positive opportunities for reform. The health consequences of loneliness and social isolation have been underestimated for years, but the pandemic has forced us to recognise them and gave governments the chance to adequately invest in addressing those problems. The innumerable losses have been accompanied by the possibility of doing things differently moving forward. 'Having things unstable for a while means that change is afoot, change is coming, and hopefully it's change for the better,' Boss said. 'I'm not sure all of this would have happened if it hadn't been a terrible emergency [that] we're living in. It's somehow opened us up in a way that is both painful *and*, in the end, may get us to a better place.'

The pandemic isn't over, but it's time to think about what kind of world we want to have when that moment arrives. What kind of people we want to be. What kind of help we offer to the vulnerable, what kind of generosity we extend to ourselves. That manifests in the way we operate our healthcare system, respond to emergencies and treat illness, of course, but it also manifests in thousands of smaller, more intimate ways. Maybe we'll be more willing to speak to strangers, neighbours and colleagues. Maybe we'll be more willing to show vulnerability. Maybe we'll change the way we approach exercise and nutrition and mood. Maybe we'll be more available for life. It is unequivocally true that this pandemic has changed us. It remains to be seen, just how much we can make of that change.

These possibilities lay on the long stretch of white sand that appeared outside my window for a brief moment in time. This morning, it was filled with people. As I sat on a bench with my coffee, I watched as they each left their towels and iPhones on the sand to catch a moment in the ocean before returning to their homes and their desks, to begin another day of work. Each of them, diving into the salt water to feel alive. Finding a small, ordinary moment that would expand into infinity. This part of us, the part that craves joy and lightness and a minute in the ocean, isn't separate from the part of us that craves for a safer, more equitable world. They are not opposing thoughts but symbiotic. The former helps us fight for the latter. The challenge now lies with the knot we are left to untangle. If we can untangle the urge to be more productive from our desire to live more – for no reason other than living is an end in and of itself – we might be able to do more for one another. If we can just hold open that place in the sun, we might be able to see clearly again.

Conclusion

Helen McCabe

I recently came across a photograph that was taken when I was in my twenties. I was sitting on a lounge chair surrounded by cheerful young men. It was 1995, and we all worked at the office of the Seven Network in Parliament House, Canberra. There are no other women in the picture. There were a handful of women who worked in the offices further along the corridor. I can't recall any of us complaining or even discussing the gender imbalance. In those days, women got on with it or we got out. I felt privileged to be there and was often reminded of the fact. That we were the only women in the place was unremarkable. Any unwanted attention we received was dealt with by the boss or political party elders behind closed doors. The discomfort we all felt from being the subject of innuendo and gossip was standard. It ranked second to the opportunity of working in the environment of Canberra politics.

Parliament House was also a competitive professional environment, regardless of role or status. Everyone was just trying to survive. There were advantages to being a young woman. Some staffers and members of parliament would prefer briefing a young female journalist over a male. It was a game, and both sides knew it. Male journalists complained about it, although they never had to navigate awkward dinner invitations. This was a more subtle challenge and on reflection, there were plenty of those. In the photo, the young men are mostly camera and sound operators. It was a complex working relationship distorted by our gender differences and therefore a lack of clarity around who was 'in charge'. There was a tendency to push back if the request came from the junior female journalist. The job was already more difficult when you account for how women are judged for their appearance, but women also had to expend enormous energy, every working day, cajoling egos to 'help' us do our jobs.

Thirty years later, I have another photograph that stands in stark contrast to the one taken at the start of my career. It was 10 March 2021. Twelve months, to the day, after the Future Women team had walked out of our Pyrmont office, leaving notebooks, merchandise and tubes of hand creams. We never returned. By the time it was safe to go back into big, busy buildings in the CBD, our workspace had relocated to North Sydney. In the photo, I am surrounded by young, bright-eyed women in Future Women T-shirts. It was taken at the end of Future Women's two-day Leadership Summit, held to coincide with International Women's Day. The women around me are unabashed, brave and ready to take on the world. The joy in the photograph stems from being physically together and from the pleasure of working as a team. And from knowing that we belong.

Future Women launched in 2018, just missing the global uprising against sexual assault and violence known as the #MeToo movement. It was partly in response to the masculine lens applied to story selection and storytelling in mainstream media. Women were still treated as almost a 'niche' audience, used as a pretty image on a beach or on the step of the family home. Future Women launched as a multimedia platform that put women at the centre of everything and spoke to them wherever and in whatever format they wanted – newsletters, interviews, columns, podcasts, books, events, and webinars. But the aim was to build something bigger – a community that was diverse, inclusive and supportive. A forum to discuss and debate the battle for equality. To have a voice on policy and politics. To be a force to be reckoned with. At the close of the 2021 Future Women Leadership Summit, the team felt for the first time indestructible. There was a sense of possibility. The fear of the pandemic had passed. We had survived it and grown. We were full of hope, ideals, smarts and strategy and we had a plan that matched our own determination and drive. For the first time in my working career, equality felt as if it were within my grasp.

After years working in the media industry surrounded by blokes – including for Rupert Murdoch – I became editor of *The Australian Women's Weekly*. The *Weekly* was a conservative, glossy mix of soft news and recipes. However, from August 2009 to 2016, the magazine controversially pursued a harder news agenda. This was my background and the brief. As print declined, the boss of ACP magazines wanted more news exclusives. We covered ageism, marriage equality and surrogacy. In a move that would have been unthinkable in the past, we put a naked fifty-year-old Deborah Hutton on the cover and later burns victim Turia Pitt. In 2010, we celebrated Julia Gillard becoming Australia's first-ever woman prime minister. We met an ambitious young politician called Scott Morrison and his wife Jenny, whose counsel would become famous a decade or so later. We released an annual power list of women featuring the first-ever female foreign minister, Julie Bishop.

But still, critics argued that women were not interested in politics. A women's magazine should stick to its knitting. And in some ways, it was a valid argument. Why would women be interested? Women had never really been included in political debates, let alone well represented. Any examination of the media shows that political stories are, to this day, disproportionately written by men, about men, next to photos from men, using source material directly and indirectly from, you guessed it, men. You can't be what you can't see and in 2009, women sure as hell couldn't see themselves in the digital or print newspapers of the time. They could, however, see themselves in the *Weekly*. It was a printed and bound room of their own.

There is no definitive evidence the decision to cover politics in the *Weekly* worked. When I started working there, 493 055 people purchased the magazine every month, and when I left, that circulation figure was 416 117, amounting to a circulation decline of around 3 per cent each year. The average decline of magazines at the time was mostly higher. So whether or not we stemmed the ever-encroaching tide of digital by going newsier, we'll never know for sure. However, there *was* evidence that if women could relate to a political issue or indeed a political figure, they were engaged and interested. Years later, tickets to a Future Women dinner with Julie Bishop would sell out faster than any of us were prepared for and she has been on the professional speaker's circuit ever since. If women are to have a more equal future, the intersection of women's media and its coverage of politics will have a pivotal role.

My optimism is undeniably linked to my personal experience of the pandemic. Yes, there was a moment of fear that our business could falter. Like every business owner, I was relieved to learn of the taxpayer-funded support payment called JobKeeper. Thank you, Scott Morrison. But I was unbelievably privileged. I say this, even as I write these words and Sydney stands on the precipice of who-knows-what: my overwhelming experience was one of freedom from the pressures of the past. The constant run of events, engagements and obligations vanished. The team was thriving in their new online environment and my life slowed down for the first time I can remember. Covid-19 was beyond my control. I could only do my best within the changed circumstances. Other aspects of my life took precedence over the ones that evaporated under new laws, and it was a welcome shift. For the first time, I was not busy. Living in Sydney, I avoided the deep and long lockdowns of 2020 that my Melbourne friends and colleagues endured. I enjoyed the slower pace of life where simplicity was valued and nothing felt rushed.

I know many women with secure jobs and incomes who also, many secretly, welcomed the slower pace. We whispered about reduced responsibilities, fewer meetings and less consumption. I felt grateful, even guilty, for the space and time. I vowed never to be 'busy' again. When the world stopped, I happily got off. I was one of the lucky ones alongside the women who decamped to holiday homes or renovated the study. But the majority of women, as Jane Gilmore explores in detail, in *Work,* were not happily finding creative ways to spend the money saved from overseas flights. The experience and fear of financial hardship spread across the country; its tentacles upended women's fragile security. Free childcare and JobKeeper helped but when things 'snapped back', this group was back where they started, only even more scared. But I am also optimistic for the most vulnerable. Policy wonks, business leaders and lawmakers are looking and listening. The pandemic opened our eyes and our hearts. It even showed us the way. And as we argue, there is no excuse for the way we treat our sick, our disabled, and our Indigenous and migrant communities.

There are beneficiaries of the pandemic. Of course there are. Every disaster produces winners and losers. There are women who will benefit now and into the future from more flexible working arrangements and more fairly shared housework and caring duties. These women will be the first to upskill or re-skill. And with employers increasingly valuing diversity of opinion and gender, they will likely be the first promoted. Author and founder of Future Fit Andrea Clarke believes the outright winner in the post-pandemic workforce is the highly skilled knowledge worker. 'These are workers who have a university degree, work for a large-scale organisation and are able to do their work from anywhere,' she explains. 'They've also been in the workforce for fifteen-plus years, so they're well networked, have credible reputation capital within their industry and have a decent amount of equity in their homes.'

Andrea surveyed 500 such people in January 2021 and found they were generally confident in their job stability. They could change roles if necessary because they have well-established networks. Andrea says hybrid working gives privileged workers the permission to live on their own terms. 'In my view, this segment of the population will benefit the most,' she says. 'Because they have enough influence in the workplace to negotiate a work arrangement that would never have been possible pre-pandemic. The benefits here are quite extraordinary, once in a generation.' A well-paid, secure job is an incredible starting point for stability and something too many women have been left without since the pandemic. A job alone, however, is no substitute for the relationships which form the very basis of our personal happiness.

One afternoon during the first national lockdown, the faint sound of 'Amazing Grace' drifted across the park and out to sea. On the balconies of an oversized square seventies apartment block, people were dotted across the facade, singing, *'I once was lost, but now am found. Was blind but now I see.'* There was no encore. Without fanfare, they retreated inside. To this day I still look up at sunset, hoping to see it repeated. Who organised it? And what happened for an entire building to sing to one another? To feel a part of a community in an apartment complex, partnership, or friendship group can provide more meaning and purpose than almost anything else in life. It is why one of the most basic needs is human connection. To belong is to feel secure. Women especially want the security of connections. Even the most fragile of relationships provide security.

In *Love*, Santilla Chingaipe explores the broadest possible definition of the word and does so from the perspective of a single person. As British philosopher Alain de Botton writes in *The Course of Love*, 'maturity means acknowledging that romantic love might constitute only a narrow, and perhaps mean-minded, aspect of emotional life, one principally focused on a quest to find love rather than to give it; to be loved rather than to love.'[126] During lockdown, love was given. It could be felt in the simplest acts of friendship and generosity. For example, my friend Kat left a painted Easter egg on my doorstep. And for a rare moment, single people were noticed. Until lockdown, they were always overlooked, especially by governments.

Families also did it tough during the pandemic but in different, often contradictory, ways. People's romantic, domestic, dating and sex lives were upended when they could either no longer see their partner, or were seeing them rather too much. Children came home en masse and homeschooling left parents wrung-out, exhausted and angry. At the same time, I spoke with parents who said there were beautiful moments during the lockdown. One mother told me that she'd never had the time and space to be creative with her child on the weekend. Normally, those weekends were jam-packed with errands and play dates and exercise classes and BBQs. During lockdowns, she and her family spent time together, using what they had at home already to stay entertained. It sounded wholesome, like she was living in a Hallmark card. And while there were arguments and tantrums and boredom and exhaustion too, her memories of that period are dominated by happy times. A soft warm glow encompassing a togetherness they'll likely never have again.

I am always surprised and impressed by how openly the Future Women community discusses mental health. This generation is more aware of anxiety or depression, bipolar disorder or OCD than my colleagues and I ever were. They have grown up in a world where therapy is encouraged and discussed. They know looking after your mental health is as critical as your physical wellbeing. This is, of course, good news when a global pandemic lands on your doorstep and the wellbeing of an entire community is threatened.

Women suffered through Covid-19 and its lockdowns differently from men. The most commonly expressed complaint among Future Women members, however, remained a crippling lack of confidence, a problem that existed pre-pandemic. Anxiety about the future, undervaluing their contribution both at home and at work and worrying themselves to the point of exhaustion, was widespread.

Covid-19 exacerbated the layered pressures many women were already feeling to be perfect in every aspect of their lives. As Emily J. Brooks describes in *Body*, anxiety is rife among women and, alarmingly, a precursor to depression. Her stories echo the conversation I had recently with a former colleague who had been newly promoted and is juggling two young children. Brooke was seated beside me at a hair salon and was clearly exhausted. We chatted about her 'perfectionism' and tendency to feel like an imposter when she's at work. I recommended she adopt my 'near enough is good enough' philosophy and prioritise sleep. I felt almost hopeful until late that night she posted on Instagram a perfect pink birthday cake in the shape of a six. This sort of self-enforced pressure reached boiling point during lockdowns and homeschooling as women who were already burning the candle at both ends, found new ways to set it on fire. The social media expectations of perfect pandemic parenting, as well as elegant working-at-home productivity, were not only absurd, they were impossible. And yet so many women aspired to them.

These women were the privileged few too. Those women working on the frontline of the virus were experiencing an entirely different kind of health dilemma. Keeping themselves safe had to be number one but many complained of being left without sufficient resources or instruction to do so. Women working as nurses or in aged care homes spoke of the anguish of not being able to give the people in their care the love, attention – and touch – they so desperately needed. Covid-19 may have been more deadly to men but it infected more women, and more women will carry the wounds of this virus into their futures. There are still far more questions than there are answers when it comes to the health impacts of this pandemic. Long-Covid has already proven to be highly debilitating and threatens the quality of life, and the mental health scars of 2020 will take a long time to recover from.

The pandemic left us all exposed. If there was a fault line in our lives or jobs, it cracked open and the chasms it created were deep and sometimes disastrous. Women lost their jobs, were put at risk of homelessness and found themselves wondering how on earth they might be productive within the four walls of a one-bedroom flat. Together we mourned the loss or loss of access to loved ones while we held little ones close and wondered what their futures might hold. We cared for our sick and stayed home to keep one another safe, and simultaneously confronted the mental health burden of doing so. The pandemic was deadly and damaging. But there were also glimpses of light. The flexible work that women have campaigned for since they entered the workforce became normal. We were reminded that the relationship we all have with our smartphone is no substitute for the people we love. And we found new ways to care for one another and show gratitude for the women and men who went to work to keep us safe.

In many ways, Covid-19 has fast-tracked the future. Corporate leaders are now more aware of the vulnerability of their employees. Future Women clients speak about ways to retain and reward female colleagues. There are people and culture managers well briefed on anxiety, imposter syndrome and perfectionism. Our most progressive businesses are experimenting with generous paternity leave, celebrating the LGBTQI+ community, better including people with disabilities and supporting staff who are experiencing domestic violence. Male-dominated industries are competing for the top female talent in order to build diversity across their business. The debate against quotas is over. Okay, well, it's almost over. Philanthropists are stepping in on mental health and governments are catching up on gender equality. There are many reasons to believe that as Australia 'builds back better' in the years to come, we will do so in a way that is more inclusive of women.

The intersection of media and politics will play a significant role in fast-tracking the advancement of gender equality. However distasteful we may find it, if the lives of women, especially vulnerable women, are to be improved, there is no avoiding politics. If my optimism for structural reform is to be realised, women will need to be at the centre of every law and every funding priority. When policy fails women, it fails society. We can't allow the privileged few to be the only beneficiaries. Women's media and women in the media were the first to identify and amplify the gendered nature of the pandemic and the policy gaps in response. Magazines may not play the role they once did but audiences are still there, consuming an ever-increasing variety of digital offerings from *Chat 10 Looks 3* to *Shameless* to *The Squiz* to *Women's Agenda*. Where once women bought a couple of magazines, today they connect to multiple platforms and discuss everything from politics to pop culture. It is through forums like these, combined with conversations around campfires, coffee tables, cattle stations and water coolers, that will see women rally together. And through our collective experiences, we can ask for better.

For a brief period in 2021, Australia opened up again. On the same week plane loads of people took off for New Zealand,

I walked through Barangaroo. The prestige strip of restaurants and office towers was heaving with people crisscrossing the road in suits and ties. It was my first 'work lunch' in over twelve months. The foyer of the newly opened Crown building was packed. A night in a basic room mid-week is nearly $900. At one of the restaurants on the water, an Adelaide-based lobbyist arrived wheeling an overnight bag. He stopped at the desk for it to be stowed. After lunch, he was straight back to the airport. What pandemic? It was like it had never happened. And perhaps this is our greatest risk. As women emerge from the pandemic, determined to build a better, fairer world, that same world might act like the nightmare never happened. And we lose our chance for reform.

Jane Gilmore, Santilla Chingaipe and Emily J. Brooks have spoken to women all over Australia and beyond its shores. Together, they have drawn a postcard from the depths of the pandemic, taking us into the living rooms of women whose experiences are both similar in some ways and starkly different in others. And on that beautifully illustrated postcard they have written a clarion call for our collective future. Their words show policymakers and members of the public alike what Australia could be. Rather than falling behind the rest of the world, we could choose to lead on gender equality. As we emerge from the pandemic, we could make Australia the best place on Earth to be a woman. Or we could fail. We could fail to take this incredible opportunity. The words of these women journalists, along with their colleagues across the Australian media, are more critical than they have ever been. As we rebuild and renew, it will be their messages of care and caution that keep politicians and policymakers accountable.

Appendix
The Gender Pay Gap

The official gender pay gap in Australia is calculated by the Workplace Gender Equality Agency (WGEA). It describes the difference between women's and men's average weekly full-time earnings, expressed as a percentage of men's earnings.

I've asked many experts why the difference is always calculated as a percentage of men's earnings. It doesn't make much sense to me. If I have ten dollars and you have twenty dollars, do I have 50 per cent less than you or do you have 100 per cent more than me? Lies, damn lies and pay gaps, I guess. Anyway, no one has been able to give me a reason why men's earnings are the baseline, other than that men have always been the baseline for everything.

The data used for the pay gap calculation comes from the Australian Bureau of Statistics Survey of Average Weekly Earnings data. In 2021 WGEA's national gender pay gap figure is 13.4 per cent. In other words, if every adult in Australia was working full-time with no overtime or bonuses, and their only source of income was the wages they earned from full-time work, women would earn 13.4 per cent less than men. Not great, but it doesn't sound too excessive. Until you start chasing the devil around in the details.

If you express the gender pay gap as a percentage of women's full-time earnings, using exactly the same data WGEA used above, you could also correctly say that men earn 15 per cent more than women. This is what the calculations looked like in May 2020.

Average Weekly Ordinary Full-time Earnings, AWE, November 2020 (Seasonally Adjusted)

Men: $1804

Women: $1562

Difference: $242

Divided by men's earnings: $242 / $1804 = 0.1342 = 13.4%

Gender Pay Gap = 13.4%

Another way to look at the same figures is to ask how much more do men get paid than women?

Divided by women's earnings: $242 / $1562 = 0.1551 = 15%

However, there is another set of data published by the Australian Bureau of Statistics that *does* include overtime and bonuses. When we use the same formula and express the difference as a percentage of women's earnings, the gender pay gap rises to 19 per cent.

Average Weekly Total Full-time Earnings, AWE, November 2020 (Seasonally Adjusted)

This is the full-time earnings, including extra payments:

Men: $1882

Women: $1582

Difference: $301

Percentage of men's earnings: $301 / $1882 = 0.159 = 16%

Percentage of women's earnings: $301 / $1582 = 0.1900 = 19%

The 19 per cent gender pay gap is more accurate, but it's still only describing the difference in earnings between men and women who work full-time. It's supposed to ensure the numbers we're looking at are directly comparable, the old apples to apples argument. There's some justification for that, but it doesn't demonstrate the reality of women's working lives. More than half of working women in Australia work part-time, usually because they are caring for children, other family members or men who claim they don't know how to vacuum. Calculating a gender pay gap by erasing one of the major factors that contribute to the gender wealth gap – women giving up paid work to do unpaid work – might give you comparable numbers, but it doesn't tell us the real difference between how much men and women earn.

Again, the Australian Bureau of Statistics provides data we can use to calculate the difference between what men and women actually earn in the time they spend on paid work. Expressed as a percentage of women's earnings, this difference before 2020 was about 46 per cent. It dropped to 42 per cent when the pandemic hit and went back up to 45 per cent again by late 2020.

Average Weekly Total Earnings (Full-time and Part-time), AWE, November 2020 (Seasonally Adjusted)

This is the average total weekly income, full-time and part-time, for men and women.

Men: $1526

Women: $1050

Difference: $476

Percentage of men's earnings: \$476 / \$1526 = 0.312 = 31%

Percentage of women's earnings: \$476 / \$1050 = 0.453 = 45%

Thus, the real pay gap between what women earn and what men earn is 45 per cent.

Endnotes

1. Statista. (2021, February 19). *Number of COVID-19 cases per 100 000 population in Australia 2020, by state* [Dataset]. https://www.statista.com/statistics/1103944/australia-coronavirus-cases-per-100-000-population-by-state/
2. Lifeline. (2020). *Lifeline will continue answering calls through COVID-19.* https://www.lifeline.org.au/resources/news-and-media-releases/media-releases/lifeline-will-continue-answering-calls-through-covid-19/
3. Gillezeau, N. (2020, July 30). Australia is living through a time between times. *Australian Financial Review.* https://www.afr.com/technology/australia-is-living-through-a-time-between-times-20200730-p55gz6
4. Madgavkar, A., White, O., Krishnan, M., Mahajan, D., & Azcue, X. (2020, July 15). *COVID-19 and gender inequality: countering the regressive effects.* McKinsey Global Institute. https://www.mckinsey.com/featured-insights/future-of-work/covid-19-and-gender-equality-countering-the-regressive-effects
5. Taylor, D. (2021, February 12). Women were let go in greater numbers during COVID, now they face being offered lower-paid roles to return to work. *Australian Broadcasting Corporation.* https://www.abc.net.au/news/2021-02-12/women-with-degrees-lost-jobs-in-greater-numbers-than-men-covid/13146120

6. Savage, M. (2020, July 1). How COVID-19 is changing women's lives. *BBC*. https://www.bbc.com/worklife/article/20200630-how-covid-19-is-changing-womens-lives
7. Women's Mental Health Alliance. (2020, June). *Policy brief: women's mental health in the context of COVID-19 and recommendations for action*. https://womenshealthvic.com.au/resources/WHV_Publications/Policy-Brief_2020.06.16_Womens-mental-health-in-the-context-of-COVID-19_(Fulltext-PDF).pdf
8. Australian Government Department of Health. (2017, October). *Medical workforce*. https://hwd.health.gov.au/webapi/customer/documents/factsheets/2016/Medical%20workforce%20factsheet%20 2016.pdf
9. TPM Builders Commercial Construction. (2020, January 30). *Women in construction (Australia): what barriers do they face?* https://www.tpmbuilders.com.au/women-in-construction-australia/
10. Morton, R. (2020, October 25). Time for a haircut and catch-up. *The Saturday Paper*. https://www.thesaturdaypaper.com.au/news/health/2020/10/24/time-haircut-and-catch/160345800010615#hrd
11. Australian Institute of Family Studies. (2015, March 2). *Demographics of living alone*. https://aifs.gov.au/publications/demographics-living-alone
12. Australian Human Rights Commission. (2020, March 5). *Respect@Work: National Inquiry into Sexual Harassment in Australian Workplaces (2020)*. https://humanrights.gov.au/our-work/sex-discrimination/publications/respectwork-sexual-harassment-national-inquiry-report-2020
13. Angelou, M. (2011, January 16). *Maya Angelou's Master Class Quotes*. Oprah.Com. https://www.oprah.com/own-master-class/maya-angelous-master-class-quotes/all
14. Ugwu, R. (2020, April 24). Brené Brown is rooting for you, especially now. *The New York Times*. https://www.nytimes.com/2020/04/24/arts/brene-brown-podcast-virus.html
15. Nyuon, N. (2020, August 9). From the wreck of the pandemic we can salvage and resurrect an inner life. *The Guardian*. https://www.theguardian.com/australia-news/2020/aug/09/from-the-wreck-of-the-pandemic-we-can-salvage-and-resurrect-an-inner-life
16. Zecher, J. L. (2020, August 27). Acedia: the lost name for the emotion we're all feeling right now. *The Conversation*. https://theconversation.com/acedia-the-lost-name-for-the-emotion-were-all-feeling-right-now-144058

17. Grant, A. (2021, May 5). Feeling blah during the pandemic? It's called languishing. *The New York Times*. https://www.nytimes.com/2021/04/19/well/mind/covid-mental-health-languishing.html
18. National Museum of Australia. (2021, May 6). *Smallpox epidemic.* https://www.nma.gov.au/defining-moments/resources/smallpox-epidemic
19. The Free Library. (n.d.) *The origin of the smallpox outbreak in Sydney in 1789.* https://www.thefreelibrary.com/The+origin+of+the+smallpox+outbreak+in+Sydney+in+1789.-a0180278188
20. Terzon, E. (2020, September 13). Victoria's 'single-person bubble' begins – and it's complicated for some singles in lockdown. *Australian Broadcasting Corporation*. https://www.abc.net.au/news/2020-09-13/victorias-coronavirus-single-person-bubble-creates-tough-choices/12658308
21. Australian Bureau of Statistics. (n.d.). *2016 Census QuickStats* [Dataset]. https://quickstats.censusdata.abs.gov.au/census_services/getproduct/census/2016/quickstat/2GMEL
22. Australian Bureau of Statistics. (2020, October 16). *Labour force status of families* [Dataset]. https://www.abs.gov.au/statistics/labour/employment-and-unemployment/labour-force-status-families/latest-release
23. NSW Government. (n.d.). *Confused about the do's and don'ts during COVID-19? Here's all you need to know on dating, safe sex, STI testing and wellbeing.* https://playsafe.health.nsw.gov.au/latest-need-to-knows/
24. Taliangis, E. (2020, May 12). Dating in the time of COVID-19: I gave it a go and got tips from love guru and break-up boss Zoë Foster Blake while I was at it. *Broadsheet*. https://www.broadsheet.com.au/national/entertainment/article/dating-time-covid-19-i-gave-it-go-and-got-tips-love-guru-and-break-boss-zoe-foster-blake-while-i-was-it
25. Marie Claire. (2021, February 5). Love after lockdown: 3 women on dating during a global pandemic. *Marie Claire*. https://www.marieclaire.com.au/dating-during-the-pandemic
26. Duncan, L. A., Schaller, M., & Park, J. H. (2009). Perceived vulnerability to disease: development and validation of a 15-item self-report instrument. *The Official Journal of the International Society for the Study of Individual Differences*, 47, 541–546. https://www2.psych.ubc.ca/~schaller/DuncanSchallerPark2009.pdf
27. Coombe, J., Hocking, J., & Biddleston, H. (2020, November 18). *Hooking up in lockdown.* University of Melbourne. https://pursuit.unimelb.edu.au/articles/hooking-up-in-lockdown

28. McRady, R. (2020, August 10). Viola Davis shows her love of 'WAP' with a 'HTGAWM' parody, Cardi B and Megan Thee Stallion respond. *ET Online.* https://www.etonline.com/viola-davis-shows-her-love-of-wap-with-a-htgawm-parody-cardi-b-and-megan-thee-stallion-respond
29. Peters, A. (2020, December 9). Are sex toys the new celebrity-endorsed fragrance? *Vogue.* https://www.vogue.co.uk/beauty/article/celebrity-sex-toys
30. Scanlan, R. (2021, April 8). The Bachelor's Abbie Chatfield launches sex toy with matching earrings. *News.com.au.* https://www.news.com.au/lifestyle/health/wellbeing/the-bachelors-abbie-chatfield-launches-sex-toy-with-matching-earrings/news-story/b5809c4ca850a413745f36b50daf3edc
31. Bell, S. J. (2020, April 28). Adult stores stay open during coronavirus as sales surge. *Australian Broadcasting Corporation.* https://www.abc.net.au/news/2020-04-28/sex-shops-help-mental-wellbeing-during-coronavirus/12189202
32. Ward, T. (2020, September 14). Sex gets complicated during the pandemic. *CNN.* https://edition.cnn.com/2020/09/14/health/sex-relationships-pandemic-study-wellness/index.html
33. Magarey, S. (2014). The sexual revolution as big flop: women's liberation lesson one. *Dangerous Ideas: Women's Liberation – Women's Studies – Around the World,* 15–24. South Australia: University of Adelaide Press. http://www.jstor.org/stable/10.20851/j.ctt1t305d7.6
34. The Local SE. (2020, September 14). *Divorce filings spike in Sweden during pandemic.* https://www.thelocal.se/20200914/divorce-filings-spike-in-sweden-during-pandemic/
35. Australian Bureau of Statistics. (2020, November 27). *COVID-19 puts the brakes on marriages in 2020.* https://www.abs.gov.au/media-centre/media-releases/covid-19-puts-brakes-marriages-2020
36. Relationships Australia. (2020, May). *COVID-19 and its effects on relationships.* https://www.relationships.org.au/what-we-do/research/online-survey/MaySurveyResults.pdf
37. Syme, R. (2020, May 5). 'This is what happens to couples under stress': an interview with Esther Perel. *The New Yorker.* https://www.newyorker.com/culture/the-new-yorker-interview/this-is-what-happens-to-couples-under-stress-an-interview-with-esther-perel
38. The Economist. (2020, August 15). The decline of the office romance. *The Economist.* https://www.economist.com/business/2020/08/13/the-decline-of-the-office-romance

39. Enquete Confinement. (2020, May 19). *Life in confinement: Investigation into an exceptional historical event: objectives and initial results* (original: La vie en confinement: Enquêter sur un événement historique exceptionnel: objectifs et premiers résultats). https://enqueteconfinement.wixsite.com/site/resultats-de-l-enquete
40. Ribeiro, C. (2020, October 9). How lockdowns are changing our friendship groups. *BBC.* https://www.bbc.com/worklife/article/20201005-how-covid-19-is-changing-our-social-networks
41. Awan, H. A., Aamir, A., Diwan, M. N., Ullah, I., Pereira-Sanchez, V., Ramalho, R., Orsolini, L., de Filippis, R., Ojeahere, M. I., Ransing, R., Vadsaria, A. K. & Virani, S. (2021). Internet and pornography use during the COVID-19 pandemic: presumed impact and what can be done. *Front. Psychiatry,* 12(623508). doi: 10.3389/fpsyt.2021.623508 https://www.frontiersin.org/articles/10.3389/fpsyt.2021.623508/full
42. Syme, R. (2020, May 5). 'This is what happens to couples under stress': an interview with Esther Perel. *The New Yorker.* https://www.newyorker.com/culture/the-new-yorker-interview/this-is-what-happens-to-couples-under-stress-an-interview-with-esther-perel
43. BBC. (2020, October 5). Why I'm not alone in missing hugs during the pandemic. *BBC.* https://www.bbc.com/news/stories-54373924
44. Pierce, S. (2020, May 15). *Touch starvation is a consequence of COVID-19's physical distancing.* Texas Medical Center. https://www.tmc.edu/news/2020/05/touch-starvation/
45. Cole, T. (2020). We can't comprehend this much sorrow: history's first draft is almost always wrong – but we still have to try and write it. *The New York Times Magazine.* https://www.nytimes.com/interactive/2020/05/18/magazine/covid-quarantine-sorrow.html
46. Theravive. (n.d.). *Persistent Complex Bereavement Disorder DSM-5.* https://www.theravive.com/therapedia/persistent-complex-bereavement-disorder-dsm--5
47. Philpot, L. M., Ramar, P., Roellinger, D. L., Barry, B. A., Sharma, P. & Ebbert, J. O. (2021). Changes in social relationships during an initial 'stay-at-home' phase of the COVID-19 pandemic: a longitudinal survey study in the U.S. *Social Science & Medicine,* 274(113779) https://doi.org/10.1016/j.socscimed.2021.113779 (https://www.sciencedirect.com/science/article/pii/S0277953621001118)
48. Grills, N. & Butcher, N. (2020, September 4). *Better engaging culturally diverse communities during COVID-19.* Pursuit, University of Melbourne. https://pursuit.unimelb.edu.au/articles/better-engaging-culturally-diverse-communities-during-covid-19

49. ABC News. (2020, July 24). Federal Treasurer forecasts difficult economic recovery after coronavirus. *Australian Broadcasting Corporation*. https://www.abc.net.au/news/2020-07-24/treasurer-josh-frydenberg-baby-boom-economy-recovery-coronavirus/12489678
50. Richardson, H. (n.d.). Gloria Steinem challenges the assumption she is an 'unfulfilled' child-free woman. *Stylist*. https://www.stylist.co.uk/people/gloria-steinem-mrs-america-how-to-fail-podcast-elizabeth-day/414050
51. Hughes, G. (2021, March 2). Parental guilt at all-time high in lockdown research shows. *Mancunian Matters*. https://www.mancunianmatters.co.uk/news/02032021-parental-guilt-at-all-time-high-in-lockdown-research-shows/
52. UN Women. (2020, November 25). *Whose time to care: unpaid care and domestic work during COVID-19*. https://data.unwomen.org/publications/whose-time-care-unpaid-care-and-domestic-work-during-covid-19
53. BBC Sounds. (n.d.). Coronavirus pandemic: women are now doing even more unpaid work. *BBC Sounds*. https://www.bbc.co.uk/sounds/play/p08zq921
54. International Labour Organization. (2018). *Care work and care jobs for the future of decent work*. https://www.ilo.org/wcmsp5/groups/public/---dgreports/---dcomm/---publ/documents/publication/wcms_633135.pdf
55. WGEA. (2016, November 9). *Unpaid care work and the labour market*. https://www.wgea.gov.au/sites/default/files/documents/australian-unpaid-care-work-and-the-labour-market.pdf.
56. Krentz, M., Kos, E., Green, A. & Garcia-Alonso, J. (2020, May 21). *Easing the COVID-19 burden on working parents*. Boston Consulting Group. https://www.bcg.com/publications/2020/helping-working-parents-ease-the-burden-of-covid-19
57. ABS. (2020, December). *Household impacts of COVID-19 survey: unpaid work*. https://www.abs.gov.au/statistics/people/people-and-communities/household-impacts-covid-19-survey/dec-2020#unpaid-work
58. Haigh, G., (Host). (2021, February 7). *The future of the office (episode 5)* [Audio podcast episode]. The Future of …, State Library Victoria. https://open.spotify.com/episode/05TsU7uhuQNGIn2AwJyJZH?si=z76QBBUOSM60XdW0pJHDDg
59. ABS. (2020, October 16). *Labour force status of families*. https://www.abs.gov.au/statistics/labour/employment-and-unemployment/labour-force-status-families/latest-release

60. ABS. (2021, June 16). *International trade: supplementary information, calendar year* [Dataset]. https://www.abs.gov.au/statistics/economy/international-trade/international-trade-supplementary-information-calendar-year/latest-release
61. Destroy the Joint [Facebook page]. (2021). https://www.facebook.com/DestroyTheJoint
62. Our Watch. (n.d.). *Quick facts*. https://www.ourwatch.org.au/quick-facts/
63. Boxall, H., Morgan, A., Brown, R. (2020, July). *Statistical Bulletin 28: the prevalence of domestic violence among women during the COVID-19 pandemic*. Australian Institute of Criminology. https://www.aic.gov.au/sites/default/files/2020-07/sb28_prevalence_of_domestic_violence_among_women_during_covid-19_pandemic.pdf
64. Women's Safety NSW. (n.d.). *Experiences of Indigenous women impacted by violence during COVID-19*. https://www.womenssafetynsw.org.au/wp-content/uploads/2020/06/EMBARGOED-UNTIL-26.06.20_Impact-of-COVID-19-on-Indigenous-women-experiencing-DFV-1.pdf
65. InTouch. (2020, December 24). *Intersectionality, family violence and the pandemic: perspectives from 2020*. https://intouch.org.au/wp-content/uploads/2020/12/inTouch-Intersectionality-family-violence-and-a-global-pandemic.pdf
66. United Nations. (2020, November 25). *International Day for the Elimination of Violence against Women: the shadow pandemic*. https://www.un.org/en/observances/ending-violence-against-women-day
67. Pearson, E. (2020, April 3). Family violence calls drop amid fear victims can't safely seek help while in lockdown. *The Age*. https://www.theage.com.au/national/victoria/family-violence-calls-drop-amid-fears-victims-can-t-safely-seek-help-while-in-lockdown-20200401-p54fzq.html
68. Woodlock, D., Bentley, K., Schulze, D., Mahoney, N., Chung, D. & Pracilio, A. (2020). *Second National Survey of Technology Abuse and Domestic Violence in Australia*. WESNET. https://wesnet.org.au/wp-content/uploads/sites/3/2020/11/Wesnet-2020-2nd-National-Survey-Report-72pp-A4-FINAL.pdf
69. Heaney, C. (2021, February 12). New domestic violence laws may criminalise coercive control in the Northern Territory. *ABC News*. https://www.abc.net.au/news/2021-02-12/coercive-control-criminalise-nt-domestic-violence-laws/13096102
70. UK Government. (2021, January 14). *Pharmacies launch codeword scheme to offer 'lifeline' to domestic abuse victims*. https://www.gov.

uk/government/news/pharmacies-launch-codeword-scheme-to-offer-lifeline-to-domestic-abuse-victims

71. Tuohy, W. (2020, May 24). Plan to help women seek family violence support through supermarkets. *The Age.* https://www.theage.com.au/national/victoria/plan-to-help-women-seek-family-violence-support-through-supermarkets-20200522-p54vn0.html
72. Andrews, D. (2020, March 30). [Facebook page]. https://www.facebook.com/DanielAndrewsMP/videos/stay-home-save-lives/218306979422749/
73. United Nations Human Rights Office of the High Commissioner. (2020, April 22). *'Responses to COVID-19 are failing people in poverty worldwide' – UN human rights expert.* https://www.ohchr.org/en/NewsEvents/Pages/DisplayNews.aspx?NewsID=25815&LangID=E
74. Australian Human Rights Commission. (2021, March 18). *Close the gap (2021).* https://humanrights.gov.au/our-work/aboriginal-and-torres-strait-islander-social-justice/publications/close-gap-2021
75. Bo, H. X., Li, W., Yang, Y., Wang, Y., Zhang, Q., Cheung, T., Wu, X. & Xiang, Y. T. (2021). Post-traumatic stress symptoms and attitude toward crisis mental health services among clinically stable patients with COVID-19 in China. *Psychological medicine, 51*(6), 1052–1053. https://doi.org/10.1017/S0033291720000999
76. Taylor, S. (2019, October 16). *The Psychology of Pandemics: preparing for the next global outbreak of infectious disease.* Cambridge Scholars Publishing. https://www.cambridgescholars.com/product/978-1-5275-3959-4
77. Savage, M. (2020, October 29). Coronavirus: the possible long-term mental health impacts. *BBC.* https://www.bbc.com/worklife/article/20201021-coronavirus-the-possible-long-term-mental-health-impacts
78. Borland, J. (2020, July 7). Low-paid, young women: the grim truth about who this recession is hitting hardest. *The Conversation.* https://theconversation.com/low-paid-young-women-the-grim-truth-about-who-this-recession-is-hitting-hardest-141892
79. CARE International. (2020, September 22). *Financial insecurity, hunger, mental health are top concerns for women worldwide.* https://www.care.org/news-and-stories/press-releases/financial-insecurity-hunger-mental-health-are-top-concerns-for-women-worldwide/
80. Jean Hailes for Women's Health. (2020, December 8). *National women's health survey 2020.* https://assets.jeanhailes.org.au/Research/2020_Womens_Health_Survey_Full_Report.pdf

81. Smith, Z. (2020, July 27). *Intimations: six essays.* Penguin.
82. Panchal, N., Kamal, R., Cox, C. & Garfield, R. (2021, February 10). *The implications of COVID-19 for mental health and substance use.* Kaiser Family Foundation. https://www.kff.org/coronavirus-covid-19/issue-brief/the-implications-of-covid-19-for-mental-health-and-substance-use/
83. Brooks, S. K., Webster, R. K., Smith L. E., Woodland, L., Wessely, S., Greenberg, N. & Rubin, G. J. (2020, February 26). The psychological impact of quarantine and how to reduce it: rapid review of the evidence, *The Lancet, 395*(10227), 912–920. https://doi.org/10.1016/S0140-6736(20)30460-8
84. *Ibid.*
85. *Ibid.*
86. Kinsella, E. (2020, September 2). As Victoria endures prolonged coronavirus lockdown, mental health workers see devastating impacts of COVID-19. *Australian Broadcasting Corporation.* https://www.abc.net.au/news/2020-09-02/mental-health-crisis-coronavirus-victoria-lifeline-calls-rise/12588500
87. *Ibid.*
88. Forte, G., Favieri, F., Tambelli, R. & Casagrande, M. (2020). COVID-19 pandemic in the Italian population: validation of a post-traumatic stress disorder questionnaire and prevalence of PTSD symptomatology. *International journal of environmental research and public health, 17*(11), 4151. https://doi.org/10.3390/ijerph17114151
89. González-Sanguino, C., Ausín, B., Castellanos, M. Á., Saiz, J., López-Gómez, A., Ugidos, C. & Muñoz, M. (2020). Mental health consequences during the initial stage of the 2020 Coronavirus pandemic (COVID-19) in Spain. *Brain, behavior, and immunity, 87,* 172–176. https://doi.org/10.1016/j.bbi.2020.05.040
90. Liang, L., Gao, T., Ren, H., Cao, R., Qin, Z., Hu, Y., Li, C., & Mei, S. (2020). Post-traumatic stress disorder and psychological distress in Chinese youths following the COVID-19 emergency. *Journal of Health Psychology, 25*(9), 1164–1175. https://doi.org/10.1177/1359105320937057
91. Wang, C., Pan, R., Wan, X., Tan, Y., Xu, L., McIntyre, R. S., Choo, F. N., Tran, B., Ho, R., Sharma, V. K. & Ho, C. (2020). A longitudinal study on the mental health of general population during the COVID-19 epidemic in China. *Brain, behavior, and immunity, 87,* 40–48. https://doi.org/10.1016/j.bbi.2020.04.028

92. Morin, A. (2020, August 25). *How collective trauma impacts your health.* Verywell Mind. https://www.verywellmind.com/effects-of-collective-trauma-5071346
93. Murthy, V. (2017, September 26). Work and the loneliness epidemic. *Harvard Business Review.* https://hbr.org/2017/09/work-and-the-loneliness-epidemic
94. Australian Psychological Society. (2020). *Loneliness and isolation in the time of COVID-19.* https://endingloneliness.com.au/wp-content/uploads/2020/12/20APS-IS-COVID-19-Loneliness-P1.pdf
95. Nikkei. (2021, January 22). 20 919 suicides in 20 years, increase for the first time in 11 years, is it due to corona? *Nikkei.com.* https://www.nikkei.com/article/DGXZQODG05BX30V00C21A1000000/
96. Japan Times. (2021, February 3). Japan's coronavirus deaths top 6000 as daily toll ties record. *Japan Times.* https://www.japantimes.co.jp/news/2021/02/03/national/tokyo-coronavirus-cases-feb-3/
97. BBC Online. (2020, October 21). Coronavirus: the possible long-term mental health impacts. *BBC Online.* https://www.bbc.com/worklife/article/20201021-coronavirus-the-possible-long-term-mental-health-impacts
98. Huang, Y. & Zhao, N. (2020). Mental health burden for the public affected by the COVID-19 outbreak in China: who will be the high-risk group? *Journal of Psychology and Health medicine, 26*(2), 1–12. https://www.researchgate.net/publication/340643259_Mental_health_burden_for_the_public_affected_by_the_COVID-19_outbreak_in_China_Who_will_be_the_high-risk_group
99. Wang, Y.-X., Guo, H.-T., Du, X.-W., Song, W., Lu, C. & Hao, W.-N. (2020, June 26). Factors associated with post-traumatic stress disorder of nurses exposed to corona virus disease 2019 in China. *Medicine (Baltimore), 99*(26). https://www.ncbi.nlm.nih.gov/pmc/articles/PMC7328992/
100. Simms, A., Fear, N. T. & Greenberg, N. (2020, June 20). The impact of having inadequate safety equipment on mental health. *Occupational Medicine (London), 70*(4), 278–281. https://pubmed.ncbi.nlm.nih.gov/32449770/
101. UC Berkley Human Rights Center and Insecurity Insight. (2021, February). *Violence against healthcare: attacks during a pandemic.* https://storymaps.arcgis.com/stories/fd6a804a17b74f0aaa3d00b76b9ab192
102. Abbasi, J. (2020, August 18). Social isolation: the other COVID-19 threat in nursing homes. *JAMA, 324*(7), 619–620. https://pubmed.ncbi.nlm.nih.gov/32692848/

103. Boss, P. (2000). *Ambiguous Loss: learning to live with unresolved grief.* Academic Trade.
104. Tenforde, M. W., Kim, S. S., Lindsell, C. J., et al. (2020, March–June) Symptom duration and risk factors for delayed return to usual health among outpatients with COVID-19 in a multistate health care systems network – United States. *MMWR Morb Mortal Wkly Rep, 69*, 993–998. http://dx.doi.org/10.15585/mmwr.mm6930e1external icon
105. World Health Organization. (n.d.). Coronavirus risk communication updates, *Update 36 – long-term symptoms.* https://www.who.int/docs/default-source/coronaviruse/risk-comms-updates/update-36-long-term-symptoms.pdf?sfvrsn=5d3789a6_2
106. Barber, C. (2020, August 31). COVID-19 can wreck your heart even if you haven't had any symptoms. *Scientific American.* https://www.scientificamerican.com/article/covid-19-can-wreck-your-heart-even-if-you-havent-had-any-symptoms/
107. Ngai, J. C., Ko, F. W., Ng, S. S., To, K. W., Tong, M. & Hui, D. S. (2010). The long-term impact of severe acute respiratory syndrome on pulmonary function, exercise capacity and health status. *Respirology, 15*(3), 543–550. https://www.ncbi.nlm.nih.gov/pmc/articles/PMC7192220/
108. Lam, M. H., Wing, Y., Yu, M. W., et al. (2009). Mental morbidities and chronic fatigue in severe acute respiratory syndrome survivors: long-term follow-up. *Arch Intern Med, 169*(22), 2142–2147. https://jamanetwork.com/journals/jamainternalmedicine/fullarticle/415378
109. Bo, H. X., Li, W., Yang, Y., et al. (2020). Post-traumatic stress symptoms and attitude toward crisis mental health services among clinically stable patients with COVID-19 in China. *Psycholical Medicine, 51*(6), 1052–1053. https://www.ncbi.nlm.nih.gov/pmc/articles/PMC7200846/
110. Ahmed, H., Patel, K., Greenwood, D. C., Halpin, S., Lewthwaite, P., Salawu, A., Eyre, L., Breen, A., O'Connor, R., Jones, A. & Sivan, M. (2020, May 31). Long-term clinical outcomes in survivors of severe acute respiratory syndrome and Middle East respiratory syndrome coronavirus outbreaks after hospitalisation or ICU admission: a systematic review and meta-analysis. *J Rehabilitative Medicine, 52*(5). https://pubmed.ncbi.nlm.nih.gov/32449782/
111. Vittori, A., Lerman, J., Cascella, M., Gomez-Morad, A. D., Marchetti, G., Marinangeli, F. & Picardo, S. G. (2020, July). COVID-19 pandemic acute respiratory distress syndrome survivors: pain after the

storm? *Anesth Analg*, *131*(1), 117–119. https://pubmed.ncbi.nlm.nih.gov/32541584/

112. See Survivor Corps: https://www.survivorcorps.com/
113. Tucker, P. & Czapla, C. S. (2021, January 9). Post-COVID Stress Disorder: another emerging consequence of the global pandemic. *Psychiatric Times*, *38*(1). https://www.psychiatrictimes.com/view/post-covid-stress-disorder-emerging-consequence-global-pandemic
114. Yip, Paul S. F., Cheung, Y. T., Chau, P. H. & Law Y. W. (2010). The impact of epidemic outbreak: the case of severe acute respiratory syndrome (SARS) and suicide among older adults in Hong Kong. *Crisis*, *31*, 86–92 https://econtent.hogrefe.com/doi/10.1027/0227-5910/a000015
115. Paxson, C., Fussell, E., Rhodes, J. & Waters, M. (2012, January). Five years later: recovery from post-traumatic stress and psychological distress among low-income mothers affected by Hurricane Katrina. *Social Sciences Medicine*, *74*(2), 150–157. https://pubmed.ncbi.nlm.nih.gov/21330117/
116. Kisely, S., Warren, N., McMahon, L., Dalais, C., Henry, I., Siskind, D., et al. (2020). Occurrence, prevention, and management of the psychological effects of emerging virus outbreaks on healthcare workers: rapid review and meta-analysis, *BMJ*, 369. https://www.bmj.com/content/369/bmj.m1642
117. BBC Online. (2020, October 21). Coronavirus: the possible long-term mental health impacts. *BBC Online*. https://www.bbc.com/worklife/article/20201021-coronavirus-the-possible-long-term-mental-health-impacts
118. Well Being Trust & The Robert Graham Center. (n.d.). *Projected deaths of despair during COVID-19*. https://wellbeingtrust.org/areas-of-focus/policy-and-advocacy/reports/projected-deaths-of-despair-during-covid-19/
119. Zuelke, A. E., Luck, T., Schroeter, M. L., Witte, A. V., Hinz, A., Engel, C., Enzenbach, C., Zachariae, S., Loeffler, M., Thiery, J., Villringer, A. & Riedel-Heller, S. G. (2018, August 1). The association between unemployment and depression – results from the population-based LIFE-adult-study. *Journal of Affective Disorders*. https://pubmed.ncbi.nlm.nih.gov/29677604/
120. Rosenberg, S., Hickey, I. & Rock, D. (n.d.). *Rethinking mental health in Australia,* University of Sydney Brain and Mind Centre. https://www.sydney.edu.au/content/dam/corporate/documents/brain-and-mind-centre/youthe/rethinking-the-mental-health-of-australia.pdf

121. Chadban, S., McDonald, M., Wyburn, K., Opdam, H., Barry, L. & Toby-Coates, P. (2020, October 20). Significant impact of COVID-19 on organ donation and transplantation in a low-prevalence country: Australia. *Kidney International, 98*(6), 1616–1618. https://www.kidney-international.org/article/S0085-2538(20)31205-9/fulltext
122. Boseley, M. (2021, March 1). Fears late cancer diagnoses in Victoria because of Covid could cause fatal spike. *The Guardian*. https://www.theguardian.com/australia-news/2021/mar/01/fears-late-cancer-diagnoses-in-victoria-because-of-covid-could-cause-fatal-spike
123. Batalu, M.M. (n.d.). The transformative twenties. The Future Laboratory. https://www.scribd.com/document/455220581/The-Transformative-Twenties-Report-Collection-pdf
124. Odell, J. (2020, December). *How to Do Nothing,* Penguin Random House/Melville House.
125. Dr Pauline Boss speaking to *Mind of State* podcast, Episode: 'Ambiguous loss and the 2020 pandemic'. https://mindofstate.com/ambiguous-loss-and-the-2020-pandemic-transcript/
126. De Botton, A. (2017). *The Course of Love,* Penguin General UK.

Acknowledgements

Work. Love. Body. was conceived of, written, and edited on Aboriginal land. We would like to acknowledge and pay our respects to elders of the Wathawarung, Dja Dja Warrung, Boonwurung and Wurundjeri people of the Kulin Nation, to the Gadigal people of the Eora Nation and the Kaurna people of the Adelaide Plains.

Future Women was fortunate to work with three outstanding Australian writers on this project. Jane Gilmore brought deep knowledge, rigorous analysis and great compassion to her chapter on *Work*. Santilla Chingaipe interwove humour and philosophy, sensitivity and soul in her chapter on *Love*. And Emily J. Brooks delivered her trademark mixture of quiet observation, honest storytelling and elegant prose in her chapter on *Body*. Our gratitude goes to each of them.

We are forever in awe of Louise Adler, a true powerhouse of the Australian publishing industry, without whose unyielding compulsion this book would not have existed. Emma Rusher was an early supporter of Future Women. It was our pleasure and privilege working with her to put this book into as many pairs of hands as possible. Thank you to the dedicated and diligent team at Hachette Australia, especially to Stacey Clair, Madison Garratt, Ailie Springall and Melissa Wilson. Thanks also to Libby Turner and Camha Pham.

Kate Leaver arrived during the structural editing stage of *Work. Love. Body.* and waved her magical wand over the book. The thoughtful patience and generosity she brings to all of her work is apparent on every page. Patti Andrews contributed preliminary designs for what became the cover, and her incomparable designs remain the heart and soul of the Future Women brand.

Our sincere thanks go to the Judith Neilson Institute for their ongoing support and commitment to quality journalism and storytelling. Their direct financial support for this book enabled us to produce a work that will shape political and policy discussions about gender equality well into the future. Their contribution to Australian journalism is unparalleled and we are forever in their debt.

The Future Women community are at the centre of everything we do. We thank them for their encouragement, engagement and enthusiasm for whatever outlandish adventures we take them on. Our thanks also go to the Future Women board whose behind-the-scenes counsel and guidance remains invaluable.

The final thank you must go to our Future Women team. Like women in workplaces across the nation and the world, they have been truly tested during the past eighteen months. At every turn, they have risen to the challenge with extraordinary accomplishment and zeal. We appreciate their tight-lipped responses every time we contemplate 'maybe writing another book?'